Life in France

PAM BOURGEOIS

Acknowledgments

For this third book in the Practical Guides to Lifestyle, Manners and Language series, published by Kolibri Languages, my thanks are due, as always, to Kari Masson as Managing Editor. Her enthusiasm, encouragement and her excellent organisational and editing skills continue to be invaluable in getting everything into shape. I am particularly grateful for her support and belief in the project from the beginning.

Stephanie Hinderer as Artistic Director contributes greatly to the overall style of the series. Her great eye for detail, creativity and constructive comments are much appreciated.

I would like to thank Christine Comte for her very professional approach to the layout and page design of the Practical Guides. She has unending patience and her considerable experience as a graphic designer is a great asset.

My thanks, too, to Garth Lombard of Largemouth Frog Productions for his work on the audio recording and musical introduction and to the talented photographers who contributed to the visual appeal of this book.

I am also indebted to Erin Tremouilhac for her help in checking the facts, to Alison Tetlow for her thoughtful comments and to Jean-Marie Bel who read the draft copy and made several helpful suggestions.

Series Editor: Pam Bourgeois
Managing Editor: Kari Masson
Artistic Director: Stephanie Hinderer
Graphic Designer: Christine Comte

Pam Bourgeois' name has long been associated with creative and effective language learning methods. Her techniques are based on years of experience running language schools for an international clientele and creating language-study materials in Europe and Africa. She has worked as a consultant in business French for the BBC and co-authored Objectifs: Assignments in Practical Language Skills (Cambridge University Press).

Pam has lived and worked for over 25 years in France where she established language schools, created and was editor-in-chief of several language magazines and developed a series of over 30 audio learning guides in three languages.

Her expertise in language acquisition and passion for cultural understanding inspired her to create Kolibri Languages and publish a series of Practical Guides to Lifestyle, Manners and Language. The guides highlight the importance of cultural awareness when learning a language or visiting another country.

Contents

		CD Tracks
Foreword		
Part 1. DAILY LIFE	*7*	**1**
Les repas	*8*	2-5
Les courses	*15*	6-9
L'emploi du temps	*22*	10-13
Les rythmes de l'année	*29*	14-17
Part 2. LEISURE TIME	*37*	**18**
À la maison	*38*	19-22
Les sorties	*45*	23-26
Le sport	*52*	27-30
Les vacances	*59*	31-34
Part 3. LIFESTYLE	*67*	**35**
Le logement	*68*	36-39
L'éducation	*75*	40-43
Le travail	*82*	44-47
La mode	*89*	48-51

Foreword

Learning, for the French, is much more than school: *L'instruction se donne à l'école, l'éducation à la maison.* [We are taught in schools; we are educated at home.]

This notion that learning is greater, more general than absorbing facts and figures is at the heart of these Practical Guides from Kolibri Languages. To learn French well enough to live in France, you must also learn about French culture, embodied in the habits of the people, their history and traditions and the slang they use to describe them all.

I've always been a firm believer that, in order to maximise learning, we must provide the most appropriate tools and the most conducive environment. These Practical Guides fit completely with my philosophy.

The photographs evoke the sounds and smells we're familiar with from our trips to France, helping us to envisage the conversations we could have and the ease we could feel once we assimilate the material. The clear layout and colour coding make it easy to find our way around, zeroing in on the parts that interest us the most, or seem most relevant to what we want and need to learn at that particular moment. The interactivity engages us, and the general knowledge entertains us. What could be more motivating?

In particular, Kolibri Languages' Life in France has enabled me to feel closer to the first love I have somewhat lost touch with over the years – the French language. I know that you, too, will fall in love more deeply with the French way of life and how to express it as you come to know them better through this comprehensive guide.

Ann Limb, OBE
Officer of the Most Excellent Order of the British Empire OBE for public service
Professor in Educational Leadership (Hon) University of West London
Former Group CEO University for Industry (learndirect)

Part 1

DAILY LIFE

DAILY LIFE
Les repas

Les repas

WHAT TO EXPECT

Meals are important to the French. Don't expect a French person to easily skip one or to be happy about having to eat quickly. The French refer to having a quick snack as eating *sur le pouce*, on the thumb. It sounds uncomfortable, which is how the French feel if they are obliged to do it. Although the legendary two-hour lunch break is becoming a thing of the past, most French people still prefer to stop work and have a proper meal rather than a snack at lunchtime.

The evening meal is a time for the family to sit and eat together. Only very young children will have their meal separately. Recent statistics show that French families spend an average of an hour at the table for their evening meal. It is seen as a time to discuss the day's events and enjoy each other's company. Nowadays, since many women work outside the home, they have less time to spend cooking than previous generations. However, they still spend about an hour a day on average preparing meals. French men often participate in the preparation and the cooking, too.

CULTURAL TIPS

The term *le petit-déjeuner* is often shortened, so you will frequently hear French people in an informal context talking about *le petit déj*. *La confiture* is also sometimes referred to as *la conf*.

If you go into a *café* in France in the morning, you will often find *croissants* and hard-boiled eggs on the counter for people to order along with their coffee in case they haven't had time to have their breakfast at home.

THE EVENING MEAL IS A TIME FOR THE FAMILY TO SIT AND EAT TOGETHER.

Life in France

DAILY LIFE

Les repas

For many families, the main meal is lunch. In rural France and in smaller towns, there is a noticeable increase in road traffic around midday as people travel home from work for their lunch. In the evening, they will eat a lighter meal, often based around a homemade soup. In larger cities, or when the distance from home is too great to allow a return journey at lunchtime, the main meal will be in the evening and will include a meat or fish course. On Fridays, as France is traditionally a Catholic country, many families prefer to eat fish.

When French people are not able to return home for lunch, they will rarely opt to eat lunch at their desks. Larger companies will have on-site cafeterias; alternatively, there are many reasonably priced fixed menus that are served only at lunchtime in *cafés, brasseries* and *restaurants*. Children will eat in their school cafeterias and university students have low-priced, three-course meals provided by the Crous, a public service that sees to the students' needs.

🔊 KEYWORDS

le petit-déjeuner	breakfast
le déjeuner	lunch
le goûter	(afterschool) snack, afternoon tea
le dîner	dinner
un casse-croûte	snack
un café	coffee
un thé	tea
un chocolat chaud	hot chocolate
une tartine	slice of bread and butter
la confiture	jam
une entrée	starter
une salade	lettuce, green salad
un plat	dish, course
le plateau de fromage	cheeseboard
le dessert	dessert
un fruit	fruit
la soupe	soup
cuisiner	to cook

Life in France

DAILY LIFE

Les repas

CULTURAL TIPS

Although French people don't take such long lunch breaks as they used to, you will still hear them saying they will do something *entre midi et deux,* between twelve and two o'clock, when they mean they will do it at lunchtime.

When young French children come home from school, they will be given a snack, *un goûter,* often called *le quatre-heures.* This is usually bread with a chocolate spread, a biscuit or cookie, or *un pain au chocolat*, a Viennese pastry with chocolate filling.

French adults do not usually have an afternoon snack. However, if you are invited to someone's house in the afternoon, you may be served tea and *des petits gâteaux,* biscuits or cookies, around five o'clock. This is called *le five o'clock*, even though English speakers would probably consider four o'clock to be the traditional time for afternoon tea.

In the French countryside, you will often hear church clocks or bells striking noon and then ringing again a few minutes later. This is because workers in the fields didn't always hear the bells the first time, and so they were rung again to make sure the workers knew that it was time for lunch.

Meals at the weekend are generally more leisurely. Breakfast may include *croissants* or Viennese pastries such as *les pains au chocolat*. Some children will eat cereal, although this habit is not as widespread as in most English-speaking countries. Adults tend to prefer *croissants* and fresh bread. Sunday lunch is usually a family occasion including members of the extended family such as grandparents. A lot of time will be spent around the table and several courses and wine will be served. It is often one of the most important family rituals.

For the French, meals are significant moments in their daily routines. Their preparation is important and they are shared occasions in family life. It is no exaggeration to say that, in France, food is appreciated and discussed and eating taken seriously and given plenty of time.

FOR THE FRENCH, MEALS ARE SIGNIFICANT MOMENTS IN THEIR DAILY ROUTINES.

IDIOMS

— *Il y a toute une tartine dans le journal à ce sujet* means there's a great spread in the newspaper about it.
— *Vendre sa salade* means to try to sell an idea.
— *Mettre les pieds dans le plat* means to put one's foot in it.
— *En faire tout un plat* means to make a great fuss about something.

Life in France

DAILY LIFE

Les repas

HISTORY AND TRADITIONS

You will sometimes see French people using *un ticket restaurant*. These are vouchers, provided by employers, that can be used to buy lunch at most restaurants or food shops. The vouchers, financed jointly by the employee's salary and by a contribution from the employer, are considered a perk, a tax-free alternative to a raise. The employer must finance between 50% and 60% of the coupon, and the recipient must be employed by the company and have a timetable that includes working before and after the lunch break. Most vouchers have a face value of between 5 and 7.50 euros.

The number of coupons that can be used to pay for a meal is limited to one at a time, but in practice often a maximum of two are accepted. No change can be given. There is no social stigma involved as they are an alternative for companies that do not have a cafeteria for their employees.

USEFUL PHRASES

– Qu'est-ce que vous mangez pour le petit-déjeuner ?
What do you have for breakfast?
– Vous mangez chez vous à midi ?
Do you eat lunch at home?
– Combien de temps vous prenez à midi ?
How long a break do you take at lunchtime?
– Vous mangez juste un casse-croûte à midi ?
Do you just have a snack for lunch?
– Qu'est-ce que les enfants mangent pour le goûter ?
What do the children have at teatime?
– Vous prenez le dîner en famille ?
Does the family have dinner together?
– Vous mangez de la viande le soir ?
Do you eat meat in the evening?
– À quelle heure vous mangez le soir ?
At what time do you eat in the evening?

Life in France

DAILY LIFE

Les repas

CULTURAL TIPS

In most French households, dessert will usually be fruit or a yoghurt, although a more elaborate dessert will be served when there are guests. Traditionally, desserts are cold and French people often find the British tradition of hot desserts surprising. However, *le crumble* has become a very popular and fashionable choice, even in restaurants renowned for fine dining.

Most French families will accompany every meal with bread. The evening meal – as well as lunch, sometimes – is often accompanied by a glass of wine. Traditional family meals include a starter, main course, cheese and dessert. A salad may be served either as the starter or after the main course.

YOU WILL HEAR

– *Je prends juste un café et une tartine à la confiture le matin.*
I just have a coffee and a slice of bread and jam in the morning.
– *Je n'ai pas le temps de rentrer à la maison à midi.*
I don't have time to go home at lunchtime.
– *En général, je déjeune au restaurant en semaine.*
I usually have lunch in a restaurant during the week.
– *Je préfère prendre un peu de temps pour déjeuner, mais pas deux heures.*
I prefer to take a bit of time to have lunch, but not two hours.
– *On essaie de manger en famille le soir.*
We try to eat together as a family in the evening.
– *Nous mangeons autour de 20 heures en semaine.*
We eat around eight o'clock in the evening during the week.
– *Le dimanche midi, on mange souvent chez mes parents ou dans ma belle-famille.*
We often have Sunday lunch at my parents' or at my in-laws'.
– *C'est moi qui fais à manger à la maison. J'adore faire la cuisine.*
I'm the one who does the cooking at home. I love cooking.

The system was introduced in the 60s and the conditions of use and attribution are governed by *Le code du travail*, French labour regulations. The coupons were intended for use as partial payment of a meal. Gradually more and more supermarkets started to accept them for the payment of groceries and the practice of using a *ticket restaurant* for purchasing a variety of items became widespread, much to the disapproval of restaurant owners.

These abuses of the system were stopped following an agreement with the supermarkets that was implemented in March 2010. The agreement limited the use of coupons in supermarkets to the purchase of sandwiches, prepared salads and prepared meals. It was later modified to include fruit and vegetables in a bid to encourage people to eat healthy food.

Life in France

DAILY LIFE

Les repas

🔊 Remember

Words borrowed from English don't always have quite the same meaning in French. *Un snack* is not something you eat, but somewhere you go to have a light meal or a sandwich.

The word for dessert in French, *un dessert*, has a soft 's' sound unlike its English equivalent. It sounds a bit odd in French if you confuse your yoghurt with the Sahara Desert!

Some words for kitchen equipment are adaptations of the English terms, so you will hear French people refer to *un blendeur* and *un mixeur*. Confusingly, when French people refer to *un mixeur*, they often mean a blender.

🔊 LANGUAGE TIPS

When talking about your own daily routines, you will find it helpful to use the indefinite pronoun *on*. This allows you to use a simpler form of the verb than the more complex *nous* form. You can say:

– *On mange de préférence à la maison le soir.*
We prefer to eat at home in the evening.

– *On ne passe pas beaucoup de temps à cuisiner.*
We don't spend a lot of time cooking.

– *On adore cuisiner, mon mari et moi.*
My husband and I love cooking.

– *Quand on peut, on sort manger au restaurant.*
When we can, we eat out at a restaurant.

LEARN MORE

You can find other examples of asking questions in *La mode*, p.89.

For further examples of how to describe your day, you can refer to *Les rythmes de l'année*, p.29.

Life in France 13

DAILY LIFE

Les repas

Most famous

Born in 1755, Anthelme Brillat-Savarin became mayor of his native town, Belley, and a magistrate. A lifelong epicurean, he is celebrated as the author of PHYSIOLOGIE DU GOÛT, published in 1825 and considered as one of the founding texts of gastronomy in France. He placed gastronomy at the centre of French culture and society and stressed the importance of the links that *"l'art de manger et l'art de la table"* created, both within the family and in society as a whole.

The influence of Brillat-Savarin on French thinking and attitudes concerning meals and food is still considerable even today. He famously said, *"Dis-moi ce que tu manges, je te dirai qui tu es."* Tell me what you eat and I will tell you who you are.

ADVANCED USEFUL PHRASES

– *Vous prenez le petit-déjeuner avant d'aller au travail ?*
  Do you eat breakfast before you go to work?
– *Est-ce que votre repas principal est le soir ou à midi ?*
  Do you have your main meal at lunchtime or in the evening?
– *Est-ce que vous mangez un repas plus élaboré le dimanche midi ?*
  Do you have a more elaborate meal at Sunday lunchtime?
– *Est-ce que vous mangez souvent sur le pouce à midi ?*
  Do you often have just a quick snack at lunchtime?
– *Vous passez combien de temps pour préparer le repas du soir ?*
  How long do you spend preparing the evening meal?
– *Vous mangez souvent au restaurant ou chez les amis ?*
  Do you often eat at restaurants or at friends' houses?
– *Est-ce que vous prenez du vin avec le repas le soir ?*
  Do you have wine with your meal in the evening?
– *Qui est-ce qui fait la cuisine chez vous ?*
  Who does the cooking in your house?

Quiz

Fill in the blanks using the verbs below.
donner, rentrer, rester, prendre, aimer, passer.

A. Vous _____ faire la cuisine ?
B. Vous _____ longtemps à table le dimanche midi ?
C. Je _____ le petit-déjeuner au café.
D. Vous _____ beaucoup de temps à préparer les repas ?
E. Qu'est-ce que vous _____ à vos enfants pour le goûter ?
F. Vous _____ tous les jours à midi pour le déjeuner ?

Answers: A. aimez, B. restez, C. prends, D. passez, E. donnez, F. rentrez.

KEY POINTS

Les repas...

- are important moments in French life.
- are eaten as a family when possible.
- are preferred to quick snacks.
- mean many people return home at lunchtime.
- are frequently occasions for spending time with relatives.

Life in France

DAILY LIFE

Les courses

Les courses

WHAT TO EXPECT

Images of colourful Provençal markets immediately come to mind when you think of food shopping in France, and French people do love to buy their fruit and vegetables from markets whenever possible. They also enjoy shopping in the many traditional food shops. However, whether they live in rural France or in towns and cities, many also shop at their local supermarket or the nearest hypermarket or superstore.

Saturday is the big shopping day. Although most small stores are open daily until seven in the evening and larger ones until eight or nine, many French people work late or have lengthy daily commutes to their place of work. They are therefore obliged to do their main shopping on Saturday. Small local supermarkets may be open on Sundays, at least in the morning, but larger supermarket chains are often closed.

CULTURAL TIPS

French people paying by cheque in a store have to show their identity card. Its number is then written on the back of the cheque. Often the cheques are put through a machine that fills in everything, leaving just the signature blank. The purchaser then signs after checking the amount.

In hypermarkets, there are several checkout lines. Some are reserved for people paying by debit card, others for people with ten articles or less and others have barcode readers where the goods can be checked out by the shopper. It is important, therefore, to verify that you are in the appropriate line. Payments by debit cards are signalled by the letters CB for *Carte Bleue*, a generic term for the main credit or debit cards in France which were originally all blue.

Life in France

DAILY LIFE

Les courses

Most French people will only purchase food for the next few days or the week ahead. Large bulk purchases are not common. The day's *baguette* is often picked up on the way home from work so that it is fresh and crisp. Some French people will purchase their meat, fruit and vegetables in their local supermarket, but many will restrict their purchases there to groceries and toiletries, preferring to shop at their local butcher or at the market for fresh food. In rural areas, people may still purchase their bread or meat from the local baker or butcher who travels around in a van, sounding the horn to alert the villagers.

Hypermarkets, *les grandes surfaces* as they are often called, are particularly popular, especially at certain times of the year such as the early autumn when the *Foires aux vins*, wine fairs, take place. Many French people will peruse the numerous magazine articles recommending which wine to buy at a given chain.

CULTURAL TIPS

In supermarkets, payment by debit card is accepted even for very small amounts, but in smaller shops there is usually a minimum amount that is indicated near the cash desk. The practice of asking for a certain amount of cash back from a supermarket cashier when paying by debit card is not current in France.

All goods, except heavy items such as packs of water, must be placed on the conveyor belt. You may be asked if you require a bag. Many supermarkets no longer supply free plastic bags for ecological reasons but will have reusable bags available for purchase. You will need to bag your goods yourself as it is not common in France to have assistants who do this for you.

When French people pay by cash, you will often hear them refer to this as *en espèces* and also as *en liquide*. The latter may sound a little odd, but it means ready cash and is related to the notion of liquidity.

KEYWORDS

l'hypermarché	hypermarket/superstore
le supermarché	supermarket
la superette	mini-market
un centre commercial	shopping centre/mall
un rayon	department, counter, aisle
l'épicerie	groceries
les fruits et légumes	fruits and vegetables
l'électroménager	household electrical appliances
le mobilier	furniture
les vêtements	clothes
un caddie	trolley/cart
un panier	(shopping) basket
la caisse	checkout, cash desk
les espèces	cash
un chèque	cheque/check
une Carte Bleue	debit card, bank card
faire les courses	to do one's shopping
faire des achats	to shop, to go shopping

Life in France

DAILY LIFE
Les courses

Saturday afternoons are for shopping in the town centres. These are social occasions, often punctuated by a pause on the terrace of a *café*. French people living in rural areas will often travel into town on Saturdays to shop for goods they cannot obtain locally.

If the market is an opportunity to meet and chat about local and national goings-on with other residents of the village or district, trips into town are a time spent with friends or family members.

Some French people may also take advantage of their lunch break to purchase an item or two. This is generally only true in the larger cities.
In the countryside and in most towns, shops close during lunchtime. In the South of France, they may only reopen around three or four in the afternoon. French people have other priorities at that time, such as eating lunch and maybe having a little *sieste*.

IDIOMS
- *On peut acheter n'importe qui* means every man has his price.
- *S'acheter une conduite* is to turn over a new leaf.
- *Se faire acheter* is to be bribed.
- *Acheter la complicité de quelqu'un* is to buy someone's silence.

Life in France

DAILY LIFE

Les courses

CULTURAL TIPS

Most chain stores and supermarkets have loyalty cards, *les cartes de fidélité*. These award points depending on the amount spent. The points then allow for coupons or special reductions. In the case of bookstores, loyalty cards permit a 5% discount on books. This is the maximum amount books can be discounted in France.

A shopping centre or mall is called *un centre commercial*. This is often abbreviated on road signs and signposts to *Ctr Cial*.

DAB is the acronym for automated teller machines, *un distributeur automatique de billets*, and GAB is the acronym for *un guichet automatique bancaire*, a machine that also allows users to perform other banking operations. Many banks no longer give money over the counter except by arrangement or at certain times. However, they have machines outside branches or in specially enclosed areas. Access is sometimes restricted after banking hours to people who have that particular bank's debit card. They must swipe it to gain entrance.

HISTORY AND TRADITIONS

The first hypermarket in the world was opened in the southern suburbs of Paris in 1963 by Carrefour. Further hypermarkets soon followed as other chains copied this new model of self-service on a huge scale. Stores were built in areas far from city centres and access was facilitated by the increasing use of personal cars. Large parking areas and petrol stations were included on the sites.

In order to qualify as a hypermarket, French law states that there must be at least 2,500 square metres of sales area and more than a third of turnover must be from the sale of food products.

FRENCH PEOPLE LIVING IN RURAL AREAS WILL OFTEN TRAVEL INTO TOWN ON SATURDAYS TO SHOP FOR GOODS THEY CANNOT OBTAIN LOCALLY.

🔊 USEFUL PHRASES

— *Où se trouve le rayon poisson ?*
  Where's the fish counter?
— *Excusez-moi, je cherche le dentifrice.*
  Excuse me, I'm looking for toothpaste.
— *Je pourrais avoir un sac, s'il vous plaît ?*
  Could I have a bag, please?
— *Je veux payer par carte, s'il vous plaît.*
  I'd like to pay by debit card, please.
— *Vous pouvez m'aider, s'il vous plaît ?*
  Could you help me, please?
— *J'aurai besoin d'un conseil, s'il vous plaît.*
  I need some advice, please.
— *Je cherche un bureau de poste.*
  I'm looking for a post office.
— *Il y a un distributeur de billets par ici ?*
  Is there a cash point/ATM around here?

Life in France

DAILY LIFE

Les courses

The number of hypermarkets in France continues to increase every year despite strict regulations as to where a hypermarket can open.

The tendency today for many of these hypermarket chains is to continue their expansion by opening hypermarkets abroad and a few very large stores in France. At the same time they are opening smaller stores in French city centres.

🔊 YOU WILL HEAR

— Je peux vous aider ?
Can I help you?
— Vous cherchez quelque chose en particulier ?
Are you looking for something in particular?
— Vous avez trouvé ce qu'il vous fallait ?
Have you found what you were looking for?
— N'hésitez pas si vous avez besoin d'aide.
Don't hesitate if you need any help.
— Vous voulez un sac ?
Do you want a bag?
— Vous souhaitez régler comment ?
How do you want to pay?
— C'est par carte ?
Is it by debit card?
— Vous pouvez saisir votre code.
You can type in your PIN code.

🔊 *Remember*

You may use *un panier*, a basket, to do your shopping, but be careful when you talk about *un panier à salade*. It's a salad shaker or basket, but also commonly used to mean a police van or wagon. So, if you hear someone has been taken away in *un panier à salade*, don't be surprised!

If someone talks about *un panier de crabes*, don't look forward to some great seafood. The person is talking about a group of people who are always at each other's throats. Somebody is *un panier percé*? It's not very complimentary. It means the person is a spendthrift. However, *le dessus du panier* are the elite, or the cream of the crop.

When someone tells you *ils sont tous à mettre dans le même panier*, it means there's not much to choose between them. Of course, you shouldn't put all your eggs in the same basket, *mettre tous ses œufs dans le même panier*, or you could be taking a big risk.

Scoring *un panier* in a game of basketball is no bad thing, and you are no doubt aware that your shopping cart on the Internet is quite simply *un panier*.

Life in France

DAILY LIFE

Les courses

🔊 LANGUAGE TIPS

Shopping assistants will often ask if you require help. You can give yourself time to look around by saying:
– *Je regarde simplement.*
I'm just looking.

– *Je fais un petit tour d'abord.*
I'd like to have a look around first.

When you want to attract an assistant's attention, you can say:
– *S'il vous plaît, Madame.*

Before paying, prepare yourself for the questions that you will be asked, such as how you want to pay and whether you want a bag. Be ready also to respond to instructions such as:
– *Vous pouvez insérer votre carte.*
Put your card in now.

– *Tapez votre code, s'il vous plaît.*
Type in your PIN code, please.

– *Vous pouvez retirer votre carte.*
You can remove your card.

🔊 ADVANCED USEFUL PHRASES

– *Vous faites vos courses surtout au supermarché ?*
Do you do your shopping mainly at the supermarket?
– *Vous faites les courses d'alimentation le week-end ?*
Do you do your food shopping at the weekend?
– *Vous vous faites livrer vos courses ?*
Do you have your shopping delivered?
– *Vous préférez faire vos courses chez les petits commerçants ?*
Do you prefer to do your shopping in small stores?
– *Vous faites quelques courses entre midi et deux ?*
Do you do any shopping at lunchtime?
– *Vous pouvez me dire où aller pour acheter un bon gâteau ?*
Can you tell me where to go to buy a nice cake?
– *Vous aimez faire du shopping le samedi ?*
Do you like going shopping on a Saturday?
– *Vous faites le marché toutes les semaines ?*
Do you go to the market every week?

🐦 LEARN MORE

You can refer to *Les sorties*, p.45, to find more examples of asking for information.

For further examples of asking for help, you can refer to *La mode*, p.89.

Life in France

DAILY LIFE
Les courses

Most famous

Le Forum des Halles in central Paris is one of the most famous shopping centres in France. Until 1969, Paris's huge wholesale market was on the site, but when this moved out to Rungis, the old market building was demolished and a mainly underground, modern shopping centre was built in its place. Over the shopping centre there is an open area that is below street level, like a sunken garden. It has sculptures and fountains. Street artists often perform there.

The Centre Commercial de la Part-Dieu in Lyon was, for a long time, the largest shopping centre or mall in Europe. It opened in 1975 and has six levels. In has since been renovated and a new area added making it the third most frequented shopping mall in Europe. Other large shopping centres can be found on the outskirts of Paris, but the Centre Commercial de la Part-Dieu is unusual in that it is very big and yet situated right in the heart of Lyon.

Quiz

Circle the words that don't belong.

A. *un supermarché, une épicerie, une boutique, une poissonnerie*

B. *un chèque, des espèces, la Carte Bleue, une carte de fidélité*

C. *pizzas, fruits et légumes, pâtes et riz, boissons*

D. *un panier, un rayon, un sac plastique, un caddie*

E. *les courses, les achats, le shopping, les voyages*

Answers: A. *une boutique* (une boutique does not sell food), B. *une carte de fidélité* (you can't pay with a loyalty card), C. *pizzas* (pizzas don't have a separate section in a supermarket), D. *un rayon* (you can't put your shopping in a supermarket department), E. *les voyages* (refers to travel and not shopping).

KEY POINTS

Les courses...

- are done mainly on a Saturday.
- are done in supermarkets for most groceries.
- are often done at markets for fresh foods.
- are not usually done during the lunch break as many shops are closed.
- are not done on Sundays as larger supermarkets are usually closed.

Life in France

DAILY LIFE
L'emploi du temps

L'emploi du temps

WHAT TO EXPECT

"C'est la course !" means it's a continual race against the clock. French people use the expression frequently when talking about their daily schedule. Indeed, a French person's day is often long and busy.

It usually involves an early start as schools, particularly secondary schools, can start as early as eight o'clock. Most offices, including official administrative services, open at half past eight and banks generally open at this time, too, as do the post offices. Traffic is therefore dense in the major cities from about half past seven onwards and buses and *métros* are packed around eight o'clock.

In the main *métro* stations, there may even be employees on the platforms to make sure that the doors can close and that people are not still trying to get on when the train should be leaving.

Before arriving at work, many mothers or fathers will have dropped their children off at school, nursery school or at their nanny's, depending on the age of the children. The majority of French mothers work, so there is usually a tight schedule to ensure that everybody gets to school and work on time.

CULTURAL TIPS

The main news on French television in the evening is at eight o'clock on two channels, TF1 and FR2. These bulletins are known collectively as *les JT*, *les journaux télévisés* or *le 20 heures*. Many French people make a point of watching one or the other. It is said that many political announcements or events are timed so as to ensure they are covered in these evening news programmes. Ministers or the prime minister are frequently invited to give their opinion on major events.

The percentage of French people attending a church service on Sundays has gradually diminished in recent years. Only about 6% of the population now regularly attends Mass on Sundays, although about two thirds of the French say they are Catholic.

MANY PEOPLE HAVE LONG MÉTRO JOURNEYS AND THEN CATCH TRAINS OUT TO THE SUBURBS.

Life in France

DAILY LIFE

L'emploi du temps

Once at work, there are normally no breaks until lunch. The French don't often snack, preferring to wait for an enjoyable lunch. The lunch break used to be two hours, but nowadays it's usually about an hour or an hour and a half. By law, it must be a minimum of 45 minutes if the business or shop remains open all day. The working day ends at five o'clock for administrative services and at six o'clock or half past six for most offices and private companies. People working in shops will not finish before seven o'clock or later.

Schools usually finish earlier, particularly where very small children are concerned, although even primary schools may continue until five o'clock. This means that grandparents or nannies are often asked to collect children from school, give them their *goûter*, an afternoon snack, and ensure they start their homework.

🔊 KEYWORDS

les horaires	timetable, schedule
l'emploi du temps	timetable, schedule
le matin	morning
le midi	midday
l'après-midi	afternoon
le soir	evening
la nuit	night
la crèche	day nursery
l'école maternelle	nursery school
la nounou	nanny
les heures de pointe	rush hour
les transports en commun	public transport
la voiture	car
le courrier	post/mail
le journal	newspaper
les infos	the news
le week-end	weekend
l'office	(church) service

Life in France

DAILY LIFE

L'emploi du temps

Peak traffic in the evening is usually between six and seven o'clock, although in Paris it may continue beyond that. Many people have long *métro* journeys and then catch trains out to the suburbs. Returning home at seven or half past seven is common for many French people, although the recently reduced working week now means many people leave work earlier on a Friday. It's time then to prepare the evening meal and catch the news and possibly watch a programme on television. Theatres, concerts and conferences are not usually scheduled to start before eight o'clock in the evening.

Weekends are more relaxed, even if some children have school on Saturday morning. Sunday is the day for sleeping in, *faire la grasse matinée*. Activities will include family meals and visits, countryside trips and various sports. Then it's bedtime for a good night's sleep before the alarm rings around half past six on Monday morning.

CULTURAL TIPS

The French sleep on average seven hours and 47 minutes per night, about 18 minutes less than 25 years ago. France has one of the highest rates of sleeping pill use.

Many French people, particularly in rural areas, travel to work by car. Several French cities have a *métro* system and many have introduced modern tramway systems alongside existing buses. In recent years, rental systems for bicycles have been put in place in Paris, Lyon and other cities and have become very popular. Users register first with a bank card deposit and then pick up a bike from one of the many stations and leave it at another station near their destination.

RENTAL SYSTEMS FOR BICYCLES HAVE BEEN PUT IN PLACE IN PARIS, LYON AND OTHER CITIES AND HAVE BECOME VERY POPULAR.

IDIOMS

– *Être du soir* means to be a night owl.
– *La nuit tous les chats sont gris* means all cats are grey in the dark.
– *Une nuit blanche* is a sleepless night.
– *La nuit porte conseil* means it's best to sleep on something.

Life in France

DAILY LIFE
L'emploi du temps

WEEKENDS ARE MORE RELAXED, EVEN IF SOME CHILDREN HAVE SCHOOL ON SATURDAY MORNING.

HISTORY AND TRADITIONS

The rhythm of French daily life has changed little over the last decade. The French sleep slightly less but spend about the same amount of time over meals. Less time is spent on domestic tasks than previously, and in general women spend less time cooking, but they still perform the majority of household tasks. Men, however, now spend slightly more time with their children. Both men and women now spend more time per day preparing themselves and getting dressed.

Over the last ten years, the number of hours the French work on average per day has diminished, although the amount of time spent on the daily journey between home and work has increased.

USEFUL PHRASES

– *Vous partez à quelle heure le matin ?*
What time do you leave in the morning?
– *Vous prenez la voiture pour aller travailler ?*
Do you take the car to go to work?
– *Vous mettez combien de temps en bus ?*
How long does it take by bus?
– *Vous commencez votre travail à quelle heure ?*
What time do you start work?
– *Est-ce que vous rentrez tard le soir ?*
Do you arrive home late in the evening?
– *À quelle heure est-ce que vous quittez le bureau le soir ?*
At what time do you leave the office in the evening?
– *Il y a beaucoup de circulation le soir ?*
Is there a lot of traffic in the evening?
– *Vous vous couchez tard ?*
Do you go to bed late?

Life in France

DAILY LIFE
L'emploi du temps

Watching television still remains the most important leisure activity, although this is rapidly changing for the younger generations for whom Internet and video games are gradually replacing the time spent watching television. The amount of time spent reading has diminished by a third.

The majority of French people when interviewed say they would like more leisure time, more time with their family and more sleep!

PEAK TRAFFIC IN THE EVENING IS USUALLY BETWEEN SIX AND SEVEN O'CLOCK, ALTHOUGH IN PARIS IT MAY CONTINUE BEYOND THAT.

CULTURAL TIPS

Suburban trains, known as TER *(Transport Express Régional)*, bring people into the city centres from the suburbs. In Paris, there is an extensive suburban train system known as the RER *(Réseau Express Régional)*.

In recent years, most primary schools and *collèges* for children between 11 and 15 used a four- or four-and-a-half-day week. This meant that they were closed on Wednesdays, although some schools had lessons on Saturday mornings. This rhythm is now considered too tiring for younger children as it involves long days. Schools are therefore moving to a five-day week with lessons on Wednesdays, but no classes on Saturdays.

Getting to a bank can be a problem for working people. Most are closed for an hour or so at lunchtime and close before people leave work in the evening. Generally banks that deal mainly with professionals are open five days a week but close on Saturdays, whereas banks which have mostly private clients close on Mondays and open on Saturdays.

Mail is usually delivered only once a day in the morning. There are no deliveries on Sundays.

🔊 YOU WILL HEAR

— Je me lève à six heures et demie tous les matins en semaine.
I get up at half past six every weekday.
— Je prends le métro pour aller travailler.
I take the underground/subway to get to work.
— J'arrive au bureau vers huit heures et demie.
I get to the office at half past eight.
— Je passe d'abord déposer mon fils chez la nounou.
I drop off my son at the nanny's first.
— Je mets une heure pour rentrer le soir.
It takes me an hour to get home in the evening.
— C'est la course tous les jours.
It's a race against the clock every day.
— Je ne travaille pas le mercredi.
I don't work on Wednesdays.
— Le week-end est plus relax.
Weekends are more relaxed.

Life in France

DAILY LIFE
L'emploi du temps

LANGUAGE TIPS

When talking to French people about their daily schedules, you will hear many slang words. The French will refer to their work as *le boulot*, their food as *la bouffe*, their car as *la bagnole* and their children as *les gamins*.

It's useful to familiarise yourself with these words, but preferable not to use them yourself. They can often sound misplaced when spoken by a foreigner and it is not always easy to judge the appropriate language register in different social situations.

When asking questions in French, it is possible to just use a rising intonation rather than changing the word order as you would in written French. This is simpler and is commonly practised by the French, too, particularly in informal conversations.

– *Vous travaillez beaucoup ?*
Do you work a lot?

– *Votre fille va à l'école ?*
Does your daughter go to school?

Remember

French people often use the word *chargé* when talking about their schedules. They mean that their days are loaded or very heavy. They will say:
– *J'ai une journée très chargée.*
I have a very busy day.

They can also say:
– *J'ai une charge de travail très importante.*
I have a very heavy workload.

Charger can also mean to be in charge of or to be responsible for something, so someone can say:
– *Je suis chargé d'organiser les sorties de dimanche.*
I'm responsible for organising Sunday outings.

LEARN MORE

You can find other examples of asking questions in *Les repas*, p.8.

For more examples of talking about the times of activities, you can refer to *Les rythmes de l'année*, p.29.

Life in France

DAILY LIFE
L'emploi du temps

Most famous

Le boulevard périphérique is the famous ring road around Paris which is frequently blocked during rush hours. Called *le périph* by most Parisians, it is 35 kilometres long and follows, for the most part, the line of the ancient fortifications around the city. It was built between 1960 and 1973.

Contrary to most roads of this nature, cars arriving from the right have priority over cars in the right lane already on the boulevard. It is the most-travelled stretch of road in France and the one most subject to bottlenecks.

The speed limit is currently 80 kilometres (50 miles) per hour, although a reduction to 50 kilometres per hour (30 mph) is sometimes discussed. This is a source of many jokes as the average speed, because of the heavy traffic, is less than 40 kilometres per hour (25 mph).

Quiz

Match the first half of the sentence with its second half.

A. *Vous prenez…*	1. *les courses le samedi ?*
B. *Vous amenez…*	2. *combien de temps pour y aller ?*
C. *Vous travaillez…*	3. *à quelle heure le soir ?*
D. *Vous rentrez…*	4. *la voiture pour aller au travail ?*
E. *Vous mettez…*	5. *près de chez vous ?*
F. *Vous faites…*	6. *votre fille chez la nounou le matin ?*

Answers: A.4, B.6, C.5, D.3, E.2, F.1.

🔊 ADVANCED USEFUL PHRASES

– *Vous faites la grasse matinée le week-end ?*
Do you sleep late at the weekend?
– *Vous démarrez le travail à quelle heure le lundi ?*
What time do you begin work on Mondays?
– *Vous avez d'autres moyens pour aller au travail que la voiture ?*
Do you have other ways of going to work apart from the car?
– *Vous travaillez combien d'heures par semaine ?*
How many hours a week do you work?
– *Comment vous vous organisez pour emmener les enfants à l'école ?*
How do you organise things to take your children to school?
– *Vous devez déposer les enfants le matin avant d'aller au travail ?*
Do you have to drop off the children in the morning before going to work?
– *Vous rentrez toujours à la même heure le soir ?*
Do you always get home from work at the same time?
– *Vous arrivez à vous reposer un peu le week-end ?*
Do you manage to have a bit of a rest at the weekend?

KEY POINTS

L'emploi du temps…

- often means long working days which start early.
- frequently requires long commutes.
- requires organising after-school childcare.
- involves long school days for schoolchildren.
- means that evening theatre and concert performances don't start before eight o'clock.

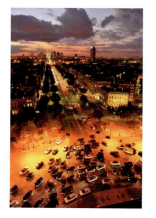

Life in France

DAILY LIFE

Les rythmes de l'année

Les rythmes de l'année

WHAT TO EXPECT

French people rush to see the dates of the public holidays as soon as the following year's calendars, diaries and agendas become available. The first of May, Labour Day, is always a holiday, but it's appreciated so much more when it falls on a Tuesday or a Thursday. When this happens, the day in between the holiday and the weekend can usually be taken off work, too. A one-day holiday becomes *un pont*, literally a bridge, and is transformed into a long four-day weekend. When this happens for several public holidays in the year, there are smiles all around, except, that is, for French employers. In some years, there can be two or three long weekends in May alone, which doesn't make for a very productive month, except for *hôteliers*!

When there's *un pont*, the roads are very busy as French people make a dash down south to the sun, to their second homes in the country or to visit family. It's definitely a time to avoid driving around France whenever possible, and hotels are also very busy. The same is true for school holidays. France is divided into three zones so that holidays, other than Christmas and summer ones, are staggered to try to reduce bottlenecks and overcrowding at coastal and ski resorts.

CULTURAL TIPS

When meeting a French person for the first time in January, you should wish them a happy new year by saying, *"Bonne année!"* You can then wish them the season's greetings by adding, *"Meilleurs vœux!"*

There is no real tradition of sending Christmas cards in France. However, the French send New Year's greetings to family, friends, business contacts and clients. These greetings are sent throughout the month of January and up to the last day of the month, but no later.

Life in France

DAILY LIFE
Les rythmes de l'année

During the summer months, there are two great waves of departures as the French take their main vacations in either July or August. While the majority of French people no longer take the traditional full month, preferring to take frequent shorter holidays, many still go away for two or three weeks at this time of year. Amusingly, those that go in July are called *les juilletistes*, and those that leave in August, *les aoûtiens*.

However, the French year is not just about vacations and traffic jams. It's also about time spent as a family. For Mother's Day, restaurants are booked weeks in advance as families have a traditional lunch together. Birthday and anniversary celebrations are also seen as a good excuse to gather as many of the family together as possible, although these will often take place in a family member's home.

CULTURAL TIPS

On May Day you will see people at crossroads selling small bunches of lily of the valley, *le muguet*. These are thought to bring good luck and will be offered to family and friends.

July 14th is the French national holiday, or Bastille Day. It is celebrated with firework displays throughout France and a grand military parade on the Champs-Élysées. Some smaller towns and villages prefer to hold their firework displays the previous day as many people choose to travel into larger towns to see grander displays on the day itself.

The long summer school holidays, *les grandes vacances*, create an important break in the year's rhythm. Although the summer break is not as long as it used to be, it is still about eight weeks. For many children whose schools are used as examination centres in June, it can be longer.

Most villages will have *une fête de village*, a village fair during the summer with various activities for children, a meal in the open and lots of music and dancing.

IDIOMS
– *Il n'était pas à la fête* means it wasn't much fun for him.
– *Ça va être ta fête !* means you're in for it.
– *Ce n'est pas tous les jours fête* means Christmas comes but once a year.
– *Faire sa fête à quelqu'un* means to bash or beat someone up.

DAILY LIFE

Les rythmes de l'année

For several days before All Saints' Day, on the first of November, the pavement in front of florists' shops will be covered with pots of multicoloured chrysanthemums. French people buy them to put on family graves, which is why this flower should never be taken as a gift when visiting a French person!

The end-of-year holiday period has its own special traditions that vary from region to region. In the East of France, *Saint Nicolas* will bring presents for children on December 6th. In Provence, the traditional 13 desserts are a much-loved part of the Christmas meal. Added to these are the many local events that are high points of the year in France's different regions. Just some of the many occasions the French can look forward to throughout the year.

BASTILLE DAY IS CELEBRATED WITH FIREWORK DISPLAYS THROUGHOUT FRANCE AND A GRAND MILITARY PARADE ON THE CHAMPS-ÉLYSÉES.

🔊 KEYWORDS

un jour férié	bank/legal holiday
un jour de fête	public holiday
un jour de congé	day off
un long week-end	long weekend
les vacances scolaires	school holidays/vacation
les congés	holidays/vacation
la fête des mères	Mother's Day
Pâques	Easter
la Pentecôte	Whit/Pentecost Sunday and Monday
le 14 juillet	Bastille Day
la Toussaint	All Saints' Day
Noël	Christmas
la Saint-Sylvestre	New Year's Eve
le premier de l'an	New Year's Day
les fêtes de fin d'année	the end-of-year holidays
partir en vacances	to go away on holiday
préparer les fêtes	to prepare the end-of-year holidays
passer les fêtes en famille	to spend the end-of-year holidays with the family

Life in France

DAILY LIFE

Les rythmes de l'année

ON THE EVENING OF JUNE 21ST, THE STREETS ARE FILLED WITH DIFFERENT MUSICAL EVENTS, SOME PLANNED AND OTHERS IMPROVISED.

HISTORY AND TRADITIONS

If you are travelling around France in June, you will have the chance to enjoy a host of musical performances on June 21st, the *fête de la musique*. Introduced in 1982 by Jacques Lang, who was minister of culture at the time, it is a celebration of all kinds of music, played by both amateur and professional musicians. On the evening of June 21st, the streets are filled with different musical events, some planned and others improvised. *Cafés* and bars are also home to various musical performances and people wander through the streets, stopping to listen whenever a performance interests them, before moving on to the next. The event has become so popular that it is now held in other European countries, too.

CULTURAL TIPS

The return to school and work after the summer is known as *la rentrée*. Leading up to *la rentrée*, shops will have displays of all the materials needed for the new school year, and theatres and television channels will advertise their new season's programmes. Everywhere – in families, in offices, in the newspapers and even in the French parliament – people will be talking about the return to work that *la rentrée* represents.

If you hear French people refer to *le réveillon*, they are talking about Christmas Eve or New Year's Eve. They may be talking about the day in general or the special meal and festivities in the evening. On Christmas Eve, many French Catholic families have a supper after the midnight Mass. This usually includes oysters and finishes with the traditional yule log, *une bûche de Noël*. There are many regional variations, notably in Provence. New Year's Eve is usually celebrated among friends, often in a restaurant.

🔊 USEFUL PHRASES

– *Vous allez au restaurant pour la fête des mères ?*
  Are you going to a restaurant for Mother's Day?
– *Vous faites le pont ?*
  Are you going to make a long weekend of it?
– *Vous prenez vos vacances en juillet ?*
  Are you taking your vacation in July?
– *Qu'est-ce que vous mangez à Noël ?*
  What do you eat for Christmas?
– *Vous partez ce week-end ?*
  Are you going away this weekend?
– *Meilleurs vœux !*
  Happy New Year!
– *C'est quand la fête du village ?*
  When is the village fête?
– *Quand commencent les vacances scolaires ?*
  When do the school holidays begin?

Life in France

DAILY LIFE

Les rythmes de l'année

 **Remember**

As France is divided into three zones for many school holidays, you will hear people referring to *zone A*, *B* or *C* when talking about the dates they will be going skiing, for example. Each zone is made up of several educational districts or *académies*. So, depending on where people live, the holidays are on different weeks. Each year the dates are rotated so that the best weeks are not always for the same regions.

If you listen to French radio or television during these periods, you will hear comments such as:
– *Cette semaine c'est le début des vacances de la zone A.*
This week it's the beginning of the holidays for zone A.

La fête des voisins is a more recent tradition. It was first introduced in 1999 and is an occasion for neighbours to get to know each other by having a meal and spending a convivial moment together. It takes places on the last Friday of May or the first Friday of June. Long tables are set up outside and people are encouraged to each bring a dish or a contribution to share. Several million people participate every year. It is seen as a way to combat the anonymous nature of many towns and cities where individuals can feel isolated.

YOU WILL HEAR

– *Mardi prochain est férié, donc on va faire le pont.*
Next Tuesday is a bank holiday, so we're going to make a long weekend of it.
– *J'ai un jour de congé la semaine prochaine.*
I have a day off next week.
– *Je prends trois semaines de congé cet été.*
I'm taking three weeks off this summer.
– *Vous partez pendant les vacances de la Toussaint ?*
Are you going away during the October holidays?
– *Qu'est-ce que vous faites pour Noël ?*
What are you doing for Christmas?
– *Cette année, je prends mes vacances en août.*
This year, I'm taking my vacation in August.
– *Vous venez à la fête du village ?*
Are you coming to the village fete?
– *Où est-ce que vous allez passer le réveillon ?*
Where are you going for New Year's Eve?

Life in France

DAILY LIFE

Les rythmes de l'année

DURING THE SUMMER MONTHS, THERE ARE TWO GREAT WAVES OF DEPARTURES AS THE FRENCH TAKE THEIR MAIN VACATIONS IN EITHER JULY OR AUGUST.

🔊 LANGUAGE TIPS

It is useful to know the names of the main French public holidays so that you can concentrate on asking questions rather than on trying to think of a translation. Many of the French words don't resemble the English names at all, such as *Pâques* for Easter or *la Saint-Sylvestre* for New Year's Eve.

Before talking to French people about the main events and holidays in their year, it is useful to review some of the keywords for forming questions such as:

– *Combien de temps ?*
How long?

– *Quand ?*
When?

– *À quel moment de l'année ?*
At what time of the year?

– *Comment ?*
How?

🔊 ADVANCED USEFUL PHRASES

– *Est-ce que vous partez au ski pendant les vacances de février ?*
Are you going skiing during the February break?
– *Vous allez voir les feux d'artifice le 14 juillet ?*
Are you going to see the firework display on Bastille Day?
– *Votre fille change d'école à la rentrée ?*
Does your daughter change schools when classes start again?
– *Vous avez vu la mode de la rentrée ?*
Have you seen the autumn fashions?
– *Vous allez passer les fêtes de fin d'année en famille ?*
Are you going to spend the end-of-year holidays with the family?
– *Est-ce que vous mangez un repas traditionnel à Noël ?*
Do you eat a traditional meal at Christmas?
– *Vous écrivez à beaucoup de gens pour les vœux du nouvel an ?*
Do you send the season's greetings to a lot of people?
– *Vous prenez combien de jours à Noël ?*
How many days off are you taking at Christmas?

 LEARN MORE

You can find more information about the French and their holidays in *Les vacances*, p.59.

For other examples of asking about people's habits, you can refer to *Les repas*, p.8.

Life in France

DAILY LIFE

Les rythmes de l'année

Most famous

France has many annual regional festivals and celebrations. Two of the most famous are *Le carnaval de Dunkerque* and *Le carnaval de Nice*.

Le carnaval de Dunkerque takes place around Shrove Tuesday, or *Mardi Gras*, in the northern coastal town of Dunkirk. Bands parade through the streets and there is much singing and dancing well into the night with everybody wearing masks and fancy dress. The carnival originated in the 17th century when a meal and celebration were held for the fishermen who were leaving for six months to fish for cod near Iceland.

Le carnaval de Nice is one of the most famous in the world. It takes place in February and lasts for two weeks. The carnival dates back to the 13th century and calls for spring to arrive. One of the high spots in today's carnivals is *la bataille des fleurs*, when floats decorated with flowers parade through Nice and young people throw flowers to the spectators. More than 1 million visitors come to Nice during the carnival.

KEY POINTS

Les rythmes de l'année...

- Many French people take an extra day off when a public holiday falls on a Tuesday or Thursday.
- The shorter school holidays are on different weeks depending on the educational district.
- Most French people take a long holiday in July or August.
- In France, people send New Year's and not Christmas greetings.
- Christmas traditions vary from one region to another.

Quiz

Are the following statements true or false?

A. In France, you can send New Year's greetings until the end of January.
　☐ True　　☐ False

B. Chrysanthemums are an appropriate gift when visiting a French family.
　☐ True　　☐ False

C. It is traditional to give a small bunch of lily of the valley on May 1st.
　☐ True　　☐ False

D. Small towns and villages often hold their Bastille Day firework displays on July 13th rather than July 14th.
　☐ True　　☐ False

E. Many French people celebrate New Year's Eve in a restaurant.
　☐ True　　☐ False

F. The February school holidays are on the same date throughout France.
　☐ True　　☐ False

Answers: A. True, B. False, C. True, D. True, E. True, F. False.

Life in France

DAILY LIFE

As they say in French

- « On ne perd rien à être poli sauf sa place dans le métro. »
  Tristan Bernard

- « Matinal. L'être, preuve de moralité. Si l'on se couche à 4 heures du matin et qu'on se lève à 8, on est paresseux, mais si l'on se met au lit à 9 heures du soir pour en sortir le lendemain à 5, on est actif. »
  Gustave Flaubert

- « L'adulte ne croit pas au Père Noël. Il vote. »
  Pierre Desproges

- « Je ne prendrai pas de calendrier cette année, car j'ai été très mécontent de celui de l'année dernière ! »
  Alphonse Allais

- « Les morts ont de la chance : ils ne voient leur famille qu'une fois par an, à la Toussaint. »
  Pierre Doris

Part 2

LEISURE TIME

LEISURE TIME
À la maison

À la maison

WHAT TO EXPECT

"Je rentre chez moi" is what most French people say when leaving work at the end of the day. Once home and after looking over their children's homework, preparing their meal and perhaps doing some household tasks, what do they then choose to do with any leisure time they have?

There is little time left, as most French people return home from work late, usually after seven o'clock. Preparing the evening meal is an enjoyable moment for many French people and is sometimes seen as part of their leisure occupations. The family members spend time around the table enjoying the meal and discussing the day's events.

CULTURAL TIPS

When a French person has a subscription to a daily newspaper, it is delivered each day with the mail or by a private distributing company. There is no tradition in France of youngsters who take on newspaper delivery rounds to earn a little money.

There is a strong tradition in France of weekly news magazines. These range from the more photograph-oriented magazines such as Paris Match to those with more in-depth articles on matters of political or social interest. They are known as *les hebdomadaires*, often shortened in everyday language to *les hebdos*. There are also several magazines about celebrities that the French call *les magazines people*, as there is no French term for this concept.

Life in France

LEISURE TIME
À la maison

Afterwards, many will simply choose to relax by watching the television or spending time online. Some will catch up on their reading with a weekly news magazine, a prize-winning novel or a political essay, all of which are very popular in France.

The evening is also the time for phone calls, in many cases to other members of the family. French people often remain close to the place where they grew up, and therefore to other family members. They visit each other regularly, especially at the weekends, and they will also telephone each other frequently. French families, particularly those of the post-war generation, are often large, so there is always someone's news to catch up on.

At the weekends, once the shopping is done, it's time to enjoy longer periods of leisure. Changes in French lifestyle have led to gardening and do-it-yourself jobs becoming popular. In the past, French people who moved from the country to towns chose to live in apartments. Now, many opt for houses within commuting distance. Even within towns, recent apartment blocks now usually have balconies and colourful displays of geraniums can be seen everywhere.

EVEN IN TOWNS, THE CULTIVATION OF PLANTS AND FLOWERS ON BALCONIES IS WIDESPREAD.

🔊 KEYWORDS

un journal	newspaper
un quotidien	daily newspaper
un hebdomadaire	weekly news magazine
un livre	book
la télévision	television
l'Internet	Internet
le bricolage	do-it-yourself jobs
le jardinage	gardening
le potager	vegetable garden
tondre la pelouse	to mow the lawn
faire la cuisine	to do the cooking
faire des mots croisés	to do crosswords
jouer aux cartes	to play cards
jouer du piano	to play the piano
jouer de la guitare	to play the guitar
recevoir des amis	to entertain friends
se reposer	to rest
se détendre	to unwind

Life in France

LEISURE TIME
À la maison

The winter months used to be difficult for those living in regions of France where heavy snowfalls were common. The older generations remember hours spent sitting by the kitchen fire during the long winter evenings. Reading and knitting were the only occupations to complement the many household tasks. Today, villages in mountain regions and in central France can still occasionally be cut off because of weather conditions, but Internet access means that people no longer feel so isolated. When people tire of looking at their computer screens, they can still resort to the many popular *jeux de société* or board games that the French enjoy playing as a family. Scrabble and Monopoly are great favourites.

In rural France, there are often only rare moments of leisure time. The many agricultural workers and farmers work long hours every day of the week. However, the vast majority of French people have more leisure time than their ancestors. But whether they live in the country or in towns and cities, one of their most important leisure activities will still be entertaining family and friends *à la maison*.

CULTURAL TIPS

Books in France have a fixed retail price and the maximum price reduction that is allowed by law is 5%. This restriction was introduced with the aim of protecting French culture. In bookshops or in chains selling books, you will not see offers of books at half-price nor buy-one-get-one-free, as is common in some other countries.

If you go around French markets in the summer months, you will see trays of apricots or peaches that are sold specifically for making jam. They will have signs such as *abricots à confiture* and will be sold at a reduced price. In rural areas of France, people will cultivate fruit specifically for making jam. Many owners of country guesthouses will serve homemade jam with breakfast.

Evening classes are not common in France. Most people have little time in the evening as they return home from work late. There are programmes for retired persons, but these are mainly during the day.

Life in France

LEISURE TIME
À la maison

HISTORY AND TRADITIONS

Traditionally, French people did not spend a lot of time looking after their gardens or yards. They cultivated fruit and vegetables for their personal use and maybe a few flowers, but the idea of having an attractive garden was not common in a rural culture where the usefulness of things was what counted. However, just as more attention is now paid to the appearance of houses, so gardening has become increasingly popular. Even in towns, the cultivation of plants and flowers on balconies is widespread.

ONE OF THE MOST IMPORTANT LEISURE ACTIVITIES IS ENTERTAINING FAMILY AND FRIENDS *À LA MAISON*.

🔊 IDIOMS
– *Vas-y piano avec le café* means go easy on the coffee.
– *C'est du bricolage* means something is a botched job.
– *Jouer cartes sur table* means to put one's cards on the table.
– *Lire entre les lignes* means to read between the lines.

🔊 USEFUL PHRASES
– *Vous lisez un journal tous les jours ?*
 Do you read a newspaper every day?
– *Vous achetez beaucoup de livres ?*
 Do you buy a lot of books?
– *Vous faites beaucoup de bricolage ?*
 Do you do a lot of do-it-yourself jobs?
– *Vous faites des mots croisés ?*
 Do you do crosswords?
– *Vous jouez d'un instrument de musique ?*
 Do you play a musical instrument?
– *Vous aimez faire la cuisine ?*
 Do you like cooking?
– *Vous recevez beaucoup ?*
 Do you entertain a lot?
– *Vous avez un potager ?*
 Do you have a vegetable garden?

Life in France

LEISURE TIME
À la maison

CULTURAL TIPS

High-speed Internet connections are the norm in France. As in many countries, more time is spent online and less time is spent watching television than even a few years ago. Young men in particular now spend an average of between one and two hours online per day.

Although French cooking is world famous with many well-known top chefs and a history of elaborate gastronomic recipes, family cooking used to consist of hearty meals often based on regional specialities. Nowadays, inspired by televised cooking programmes and competitions, cooking has also become a hobby. That this has led to as many passionate participants as well-informed critics is not surprising in a culture where food and its preparation have always been of major importance.

Much of French people's leisure time is given to entertaining. This is often for close family, whereas meals with friends are often in restaurants.

Garden centres, as opposed to the more traditional stores for agricultural needs, can now be found even in town centres and all offer a huge selection of plants and shrubs.

Similarly, until recently, animals were not considered as pets in rural areas. Most households had at least a dog, but the dog remained outside and guarded the property. Cats were kept to avoid mice and again were often not allowed into the house. Nowadays, there is a thriving industry in France in pet food and care.

Many families living in the French countryside used to spend free time in their kitchen sitting around the table or in front of an open fire. They would seldom sit in a comfortable armchair in a separate living room. Callers would also be welcomed into the kitchen and invited to sit around the table. Now, unexpected visitors may still be invited to sit around the table, but it will usually be in the main living area rather than in the kitchen.

🔊 YOU WILL HEAR

– *Vous voulez lire le journal ?*
Do you want to read the newspaper?
– *Vous voulez regarder la télévision ?*
Do you want to watch television?
– *Ça vous dit de jouer aux cartes ?*
Would you like to play a game of cards?
– *Il faut que je tonde la pelouse.*
I have to mow the lawn.
– *Je vais faire de la confiture avec ces abricots.*
I'm going to make jam with these apricots.
– *J'ai un peu de bricolage à faire.*
I have a few odd jobs to do.
– *Je vais lire au jardin.*
I'm going to read in the garden.
– *Je vais me reposer un petit moment.*
I'm going to have a little rest.

Life in France

LEISURE TIME
À la maison

 LANGUAGE TIPS

When talking about what they do in their leisure time, French people may want to compare what they used to do to what they do now.

When talking about their current habits, French people will use the simple present:
– *Quand je rentre du travail, je lis le journal avant le dîner.*
When I get home from work, I read the newspaper before dinner.

When they are talking about what they used to do in the past, they will use the imperfect tense. They will say:
– *Quand j'étais enfant, on passait nos soirées dans la cuisine.*
When I was a child, we spent our evenings in the kitchen.

 *Remember*

When talking about everyday leisure activities in the home, be careful to avoid some easily made errors.

If you are talking about books, the word in French is masculine, *un livre*. *Une livre* is a pound in weight.

To say you have seen a programme on the television, make sure you use *à la télévision*. *Sur la télévision* is for something that is literally on top of the television set or screen.

When talking about playing cards or games, you need to use *au, à la* or *aux* depending on the gender and quantity of the following noun, as in:
– *J'aime jouer aux cartes.*
I like playing cards.

However, when talking about playing a musical instrument, you should use *du, de la* or *des* as in:
– *J'adore jouer du piano.*
I love playing the piano.

 ADVANCED USEFUL PHRASES

– *Vous préférez lire un hebdomadaire ou un quotidien ?*
  Do you prefer reading a weekly news magazine or a daily newspaper?
– *Vous regardez les actualités à la télévision ?*
  Do you watch the news on television?
– *Est-ce que vous achetez les romans qui ont gagné les prix littéraires ?*
  Do you buy the novels that have won the literary prizes?
– *Est-ce que vous passez du temps sur Internet chez vous le soir ?*
  Do you spend time online at home in the evening?
– *C'est vous ou votre femme qui entretient le jardin ?*
  Is it you or your wife who does the gardening?
– *Ce sont les légumes de votre jardin dans le potage ?*
  Are the vegetables in the soup from your garden?
– *J'aimerais beaucoup vous entendre jouer du piano.*
  I'd love to hear you play the piano.
– *Vous êtes plus doué que moi pour jouer de la guitare.*
  You're more gifted than I am at playing the guitar.

 LEARN MORE

For more examples of enquiring about people's habits, you can refer to *Les repas*, p.8.

You can refer to *Les vacances*, p.59, for further examples of people talking about future plans.

Life in France

LEISURE TIME
À la maison

Most famous

In France, autumn is the season for prestigious literary prizes, and in many people's homes you will find copies of the books that have won the year's prizes. Most bookshops and the *Salon du Livre* have prominent displays of these prize-winning books. Traditionally they have simple cream covers without illustrations. Red bands around the books indicate which prize they have won.

The most famous prize is *le prix Goncourt*. It was created in 1903 and is awarded with much fanfare at the beginning of November. The prize winner is chosen by ten judges who meet on the first Tuesday of each month in a room over the *restaurant Drouant* in Paris. The prize money is a purely symbolic ten euros. However, the subsequent renown ensures that the novel quickly becomes a bestseller. Celebrated authors who have won *le prix Goncourt* include Marcel Proust, André Malraux and Simone de Beauvoir.

Among other famous French literary prizes are *le prix Renaudot, le prix Médicis, le prix Femina* and *le grand prix du roman de l'Académie française*.

Quiz

Fill in the blanks using the word bank below.
confiture, prix, bricolage, journal, fêtes, instrument

A. *Quel est votre _____ de musique préféré ?*
B. *Vous recevez un _____ tous les jours ?*
C. *Vous faites de la _____ l'été ?*
D. *Vous partez pour les _____ de fin d'année ?*
E. *Est-ce que vous aimez faire du _____ ?*
F. *Vous achetez les livres qui ont gagné les _____ littéraires ?*

Answers: A. instrument, B. journal, C. confiture, D. fêtes, E. bricolage, F. prix.

KEY POINTS

À la maison...

- French people spend a lot of their leisure time entertaining family members.
- the French spend more time doing odd jobs than in the past.
- newspapers are delivered by mail or a private distributing company.
- there is a tradition of cultivating vegetable gardens and making jam.
- the vast majority of Internet connections are high-speed.

Life in France

LEISURE TIME
Les sorties

Les sorties

WHAT TO EXPECT

The French are passionate about culture, particularly their own! They believe that they need to protect their distinctive artistic productions and applaud government support for the arts. Many fear that the French language will lose its place in the world if creative expression in French is not given a helping hand.

Over the years, various measures have been introduced to ensure that the French language and culture are preserved. As well as legislation concerning the retail prices of books, French television channels must, by law, subsidise French cinema productions. A special status is given to people working in the arts allowing them to be paid, under certain conditions, during periods when they have no work. Young people are encouraged and given incentives to go to the theatre, visit museums and purchase books. There are numerous strategies to protect the French language from the encroachment of English.

An example of how attached the French are to their history and culture is seen every year during *Les journées du patrimoine*. On the third weekend in September, museums, *châteaux*, town halls and countless other examples of French architecture and culture are open to the public for free. Millions of French people participate and every year the success of this initiative can be measured not only by the crowds but also by the interest and pride it stimulates.

CULTURAL TIPS

Most museums in France are closed on Tuesdays and most public holidays, but they are open every other day of the week, including Sundays. National museums are usually free on the first Sunday of every month. The permanent exhibitions in some national museums are free all the time to encourage young people to visit.

If you go to a theatre performance or concert in France, you will need to follow the signs for *les numéros pairs* or *les numéros impairs* depending upon whether your seat has an even or odd number. You will then need to look for your row, *la rangée*.

Life in France

LEISURE TIME

Les sorties

During the rest of the year, many French people choose to visit museums and art exhibitions as well as going to theatre performances and concerts. This is particularly true during school holiday periods when grandparents accompany their grandchildren on such visits. A rainy day during family holidays will similarly ensure that France's many regional museums will be particularly busy. Many French families feel they have a duty to equip their children with an awareness of their regional and national identity and also an understanding of important historical and cultural events.

Of course, the busy working week and long school days mean that outings during the week are often limited. Most performances start

CULTURAL TIPS

In June, many theatres and concert halls will start selling season tickets, *les abonnements*. French people will select the performances they want to see during the season and pay for them in advance. Usually it is necessary to choose at least four performances to obtain the reduced rates of a season ticket. The best seats are given to season ticket holders, but the number of seats sold this way is limited and, in September, people who may want tickets for just one or two performances can purchase the remaining seats.

When the French refer to the cinema in an informal manner, they often talk about *le cinoche*.

THE FRENCH BELIEVE THAT THEY NEED TO PROTECT THEIR DISTINCTIVE ARTISTIC PRODUCTIONS AND APPLAUD GOVERNMENT SUPPORT FOR THE ARTS.

IDIOMS

– *Elle fait tout un cinéma* means it's all an act.
– *C'est du théâtre* means it's just playacting.
– *Être aux premières loges* means to have a ringside seat.
– *Elle a dû laisser sa fierté au vestiaire* means he had to put aside his pride.

Life in France

LEISURE TIME
Les sorties

at eight in the evening to allow for the fact that people often return home late. Not all families have the budgets to permit many outings, either. Others will prefer a meal out or an evening with family or friends. However, there is a general belief that cultural outings are important and that these activities should be encouraged.

None of this stops the French from going to see the latest Hollywood blockbuster, but they will also go to see French films and are particularly pleased when a French film earns international recognition. Above all, they feel that French culture, whether expressed through film, music or literature, has its own particular and valuable tradition and that, as with French cuisine, it defines who they are and what makes them unique.

🔊 USEFUL PHRASES

– *Pour deux personnes, s'il vous plaît.*
  For two, please.
– *C'est bien en VO, n'est-ce pas ?*
  It's the English/original version, isn't it?
– *C'est combien la place ?*
  How much is the ticket?
– *Il vous reste des places pour ce soir ?*
  Do you have any seats left for tonight?
– *Ce sont des places au balcon ?*
  Are they seats in the dress circle/mezzanine?
– *Vous avez le programme, s'il vous plaît ?*
  Do you have the programme, please?
– *Le spectacle commence à quelle heure ?*
  What time does the performance begin?
– *Il y a un vestiaire, s'il vous plaît ?*
  Is there a cloakroom/coatroom, please?

🔊 KEYWORDS

un cinéma	cinema, movie theater
un théâtre	theatre
un musée	museum
un spectacle	show
une exposition	exhibition, show
une conférence	lecture, talk
une séance	performance, showing, film
un entracte	interval, intermission
une bande-annonce	trailer
une pièce de théâtre	play
l'orchestre	stalls, orchestra
le balcon	dress circle, mezzanine
le deuxième balcon	upper circle/balcony
le guichet	box office, ticket office
un vestiaire	cloakroom/coatroom
un abonnement	season ticket
applaudir	to applaud, clap
faire la queue	to queue, stand in line

Life in France

LEISURE TIME
Les sorties

CULTURAL TIPS

When French people appreciate a performance, the applause at the end will rapidly become rhythmic so that everybody in the audience is clapping in harmony at the same speed. This will continue, indicating that the audience wants more, until the artists reappear and perform an encore. It may then be repeated until there is a further encore. It is only when the house lights are switched on that the clapping will fade.

Cinema programmes in France change on Wednesdays. This is because, currently, many French children don't attend school on Wednesdays. Previously, when Thursday was the free day for schoolchildren, the programmes changed on Thursdays. The new releases of the week are therefore announced on Tuesday evenings at the end of news programmes and on Wednesday mornings on the radio.

HISTORY AND TRADITIONS

It was traditional until the late 1970s to be shown to your seat in a French cinema by a woman with a torch or flashlight. This person was called *une ouvreuse* and it was customary to give a tip when she found you a seat. The *ouvreuse* would also sell ice-cream during the intermission. When cinemas started to introduce separate showings at particular times rather than continuous programmes, there was no longer a need for these persons as the house lights were raised between films.

Le théâtre de boulevard originated in late 18th-century Paris in the theatres that opened along the boulevard du Temple. This popular form of theatre, based on pantomime and acrobatic feats, contrasted with the theatre of the upper classes. During the Second Empire, it evolved into melodrama and vaudeville. It has changed little since and is still popular despite its timeworn conventions. Today, *le théâtre de boulevard* is used to describe a form of commercial theatre that doesn't aim to be innovative.

🔊 YOU WILL HEAR

— *Elle joue très bien.*
  She acts really well.
— *C'est un spectacle magnifique.*
  It's a fantastic show.
— *Ça vaut vraiment le coup de venir voir cette exposition.*
  It's really worth coming to see this exhibition.
— *Demain soir, nous allons au théâtre.*
  Tomorrow evening, we're going to the theatre.
— *J'ai vu la bande-annonce et il a l'air très bien.*
  I've seen the trailer and it looks really good.
— *Le spectacle LES MISÉRABLES joue à guichets fermés.*
  LES MISÉRABLES is fully booked.
— *Je crois que ça sort en salle bientôt.*
  I think it will be released soon.
— *J'ai une super place dans la troisième rangée.*
  I've got a great seat in the third row.

LEISURE TIME

Les sorties

🔊 Remember

French people talk about *une salle de spectacle,* or simply *la salle*, when they are referring to the place that houses a performance, whether it be a film or a live performance. However, the French also use *la salle* to mean the public or audience, as in:
– *La salle a beaucoup applaudi.*
The audience clapped a lot.

Similarly, the sign *Sortie* indicates the way out in a theatre and *la sortie des artistes* is specifically the stage door. However, *une sortie* can also be an outing or, when referring to the evening, a night out, as in:
– *Nous allons faire une petite sortie dimanche.*
We're going on a little outing on Sunday.

– *Samedi, nous sommes de sortie.*
We're having a night out on Saturday.

Films in a foreign language that are not dubbed, or films seen as more experimental in nature, can still be seen in small cinemas known collectively as *les cinémas d'art et d'essai*. Today, these cinemas are subsidised to help encourage independent filmmakers. About a quarter of cinema tickets sold in France are for these cinemas. They show European films and French films in particular.

🔊 ADVANCED USEFUL PHRASES

– *À quelle heure est la dernière séance, s'il vous plaît ?*
When is the last show, please?
– *Est-ce qu'il reste de bonnes places pour vendredi soir ?*
Are there any good seats left for Friday evening?
– *À quelle heure faut-il arriver pour prendre les billets ?*
What time do we need to come to pick up the tickets?
– *Il faut compter combien de temps pour faire le tour du musée ?*
How long does it take to go around the museum?
– *Quand se termine l'exposition temporaire ?*
When does the temporary exhibition finish?
– *Il faut faire la queue pendant combien de temps ?*
How long do you have to wait in line?
– *J'aimerais voir l'exposition actuelle.*
I'd like to see the current exhibition.
– *Où est-ce que je peux acheter des billets pour ce spectacle ?*
Where can I buy tickets for this show?

Life in France

LEISURE TIME

Les sorties

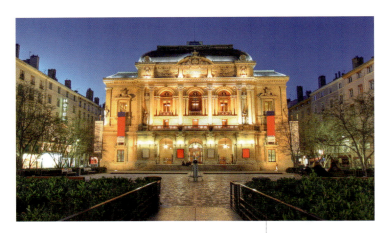

CULTURAL TIPS

When you go to see a foreign film in France, you should check whether, after the title, the letters VF or VO appear. The former indicates that it is the French version and that the dialogue will be dubbed in French. When a film is marked VO, it means it is the *version originale* and French subtitles will have been added.

You will probably find that performances, other than films, will not start exactly on time in France but about 10 or 15 minutes late. The French mockingly call this *le petit quart d'heure*, which is their way of affectionately accepting this.

IN JUNE, MANY THEATRES AND CONCERT HALLS WILL START SELLING SEASON TICKETS, *LES ABONNEMENTS*.

 LANGUAGE TIPS

When you go to visit a famous place or a museum, you can use the verb *visiter*:
– *J'ai visité le Louvre quand je suis allé à Paris.*
I visited the Louvre when I was in Paris.

However, when you visit a person you should use the expression *rendre visite*:
– *Je suis allée rendre visite à ma tante hier.*
I went to visit my aunt yesterday.

When talking about the release of a new film, you will need to ask:
– *Quand est-ce que ce film va sortir en salle ?*
When will this film be in cinemas?

If you want to know at what time a particular film is showing, you should ask:
– *C'est à quelle heure la prochaine séance ?*
When is the next showing?

 LEARN MORE

You can find other examples of asking about the times of activities in *L'emploi du temps*, p.22.

For further examples of asking for information, you can refer to *Les courses*, p.15.

Life in France

LEISURE TIME
Les sorties

Most famous

The oldest and most famous music hall in Paris is the Olympia. It was founded by the creator of the Moulin Rouge and opened in 1889. The building has an eye-catching façade and red interior. It was completely restored after the French government decided to preserve the building when it was threatened with demolition. The renovated Olympia was inaugurated in 1997. Among famous stars who have performed there are Edith Piaf, Marlene Dietrich, Charles Aznavour, Jacques Brel and Johnny Hallyday.

Le Grand Rex is a legendary cinema and the largest in Paris. Built in Art Deco style, it opened in 1932. In 1981, it was classed as a national monument by the French government. The cinema's main screen covers 300 square metres, making it the largest in France. Visitors can take a guided tour of the cinema, learn about its history, admire the high, imposing ceiling and go behind the enormous screen.

Quiz

Put the following dialogue in the correct order.

A. *Il y en a une qui vient de commencer, mais le film n'a pas encore démarré.*
B. *Alors je préfère attendre la séance d'après.*
C. *C'est bien ça.*
D. *Donc deux places pour la séance de vingt heures dix ?*
E. *Je voudrais deux places, s'il vous plaît.*
F. *Ce sera les rangées complètement devant.*
G. *Oui, pour quelle séance ?*
H. *Il reste des places ?*
I. *Merci. Bonne soirée.*
J. *Ça vous fait dix-huit euros.*
K. *Tenez.*
L. *La prochaine est à quelle heure ?*

Answers: E, G, L, A, H, F, B, D, C, J, K, I.

KEY POINTS

Les sorties...

- include visits to museums and historical monuments.
- are scheduled to start at eight o'clock or later.
- include meals with family and friends.
- involve cultural activities when possible.
- are encouraged by measures to promote French culture.

Life in France

LEISURE TIME
Le sport

Le sport

WHAT TO EXPECT

Go to any park in France on a Sunday afternoon and from about three o'clock onwards, once Sunday lunch is over, you will see families out for a stroll. You will also see many French people out walking in the countryside. Young and old make the trip out of the cities and spend an hour or two enjoying the views, the fresh air and the exercise.

In France, mayors of larger towns often make it a priority to create paths alongside the main rivers, replacing parking areas and allowing for extended walks that are protected from the traffic. In Lyon, for example, it is now possible to walk for several kilometres following the Rhône river through the city. At weekends, the riverside is thronged with walkers and the banks of the Saône, which also runs through Lyon, are being adapted to create yet more paths.

CULTURAL TIPS

When French schoolchildren take their final year exam, *le baccalauréat*, there is a mark (out of 20) for sport. This is based on a continuous assessment of performance in two or three sports. The final mark is then included in the calculation of the average overall grade in all subjects and contributes, therefore, to the candidate passing or failing the exam.

If a French person talks about *les vêtements sport*, they are referring to casual dress or clothing and not sportswear. *Les vêtements de sport* is the term used to refer specifically to sportswear.

IN LYON, IT IS NOW POSSIBLE TO WALK FOR SEVERAL KILOMETRES FOLLOWING THE RHÔNE RIVER THROUGH THE CITY.

Life in France

LEISURE TIME

Le sport

In the countryside, there are multitudes of possibilities for those who enjoy more challenging walks and hikes. Numerous well-signposted trails, ranging from short country walks to long-distance footpaths, *les sentiers de grandes randonnées*, called familiarly *les GR* by the French, allow walkers to explore the varied regions of France on foot. Hiking, *randonner*, is one of the preferred sports of the French as the number of walkers on these routes, particularly during the summer months, amply demonstrates.

Of course no hiker in the countryside could fail to notice the number of cyclists on French country roads. This is a sport taken very seriously in France and cyclists, wearing cycling helmets and the latest cycling shorts, rush past taking steep inclines in their stride. Le Tour de France is no doubt one of the reasons for the popularity of cycling, but there is a long tradition of cycling in France and there are many races on a smaller scale and many cycling clubs.

 KEYWORDS

un moniteur	instructor
un sac à dos	rucksack/backpack
les baskets	trainers/sneakers
les chaussures de marche	walking shoes
une raquette	racket
les vêtements de sport	sportswear
un short	a pair of shorts
un tee-shirt	T-shirt
un maillot	T-shirt, jersey
marcher	to walk
se balader	to go for a walk
skier	to ski
nager	to swim
jouer au tennis	to play tennis
faire du vélo	to cycle
faire du footing	to go jogging
être en forme	to be fit
garder la ligne	to keep one's figure

IDIOMS

– *On marche sur la tête* means that something is crazy.
– *Avoir un petit vélo dans la tête* means to be not all there.
– *Lâche-moi les baskets !* means "Get off my back!"
– *Nager entre deux eaux* means not to commit oneself.

Life in France

LEISURE TIME

Le sport

CULTURAL TIPS

When French people go hiking, you will often hear them talk about *le dénivelé* of the path they have taken. This is the difference in height, measured in metres, between the lowest and the highest points on the trail. Combined with the length of the walk, it indicates the degree of difficulty. It is an important concept for French walkers. Cross-country skiers also use this measurement.

French tennis player Yannick Noah and footballer Zinedine Zidane have long been high on the list of the 50 most popular French personalities, which is published twice yearly. Noah has held the number one position several times, including for five uninterrupted years from 2007 to 2012.

One of the other great national sports is, unsurprisingly, skiing. A week spent skiing is part of the traditional winter programme for many French families. Roads to and from the many skiing resorts in the Alps and the Pyrenees are busy throughout the period, and the television weather forecasts give abundant information about the quality and quantity of snow. Those that are fortunate enough to live within easy reach of skiing areas will pop on their skis most winter weekends.

Football, or soccer, rugby, tennis and increasingly golf are all highly popular, although watching takes priority over participating for some. The more extreme sports also have their fans. You can watch the gliders skim over the cliffs and the kite-surfers skim the waves in many parts of France, but the majority of French people will prefer their local gym to attempting to compete in such sports. And then there is always *pétanque*. What more typically French way to enjoy an afternoon in the open, shaded by the traditional plane trees, than rolling steel balls, *boules*, to try and hit a small wooden ball on the dusty surface of the village square?

USEFUL PHRASES

– *J'aime bien me balader.*
   I really enjoy walking.
– *Vous skiez ?*
   Do you ski?
– *Vous allez nager à la piscine toutes les semaines ?*
   Do you go swimming at the pool every week?
– *J'adore jouer au tennis.*
   I love playing tennis.
– *Je n'ai pas de chaussures de marche avec moi.*
   I don't have any walking shoes with me.
– *Je vais mettre un short si on va marcher.*
   I'll go and put on a pair of shorts if we're going for a walk.
– *Vous êtes très en forme.*
   You're very fit.
– *Vous allez régulièrement à la gym ?*
   Do you go to the gym regularly?

Life in France

LEISURE TIME

Le sport

HIKING, *RANDONNER*, IS ONE OF THE PREFERRED SPORTS OF THE FRENCH.

HISTORY AND TRADITIONS

There is a long tradition in France of voluntary or professional organisations and the State working together to promote excellence in sports.

Originally, mountain guides accompanying individuals and groups of people through the dangerous mountain terrains came from voluntary and then professional organisations. In the 1940s, national diplomas were introduced, *les diplômes d'État*. In 1975, further rules were introduced and soon after more specialised diplomas created. Today it is essential to have an appropriate diploma to be allowed to instruct and accompany members of the public. However, even though the State regulates these qualifications, it is the professional union of mountain guides that establishes the practices and obligations of the profession with respect to the client, and once qualified, most guides choose to work independently in small local groupings.

🔊 YOU WILL HEAR

— *Vous savez skier ?*
  Do you know how to ski?
— *Vous aimez marcher ?*
  Do you enjoy walking?
— *Je fais du vélo tous les week-ends.*
  I go cycling every weekend.
— *Je préfère nager dans la mer qu'à la piscine.*
  I prefer swimming in the sea to in a swimming pool.
— *J'essaie de rester en forme.*
  I try to stay fit.
— *Vous avez des baskets avec vous ?*
  Do you have trainers/sneakers with you?
— *Je peux vous prêter un sac à dos.*
  I can lend you a rucksack/backpack.
— *Je vais faire du footing au parc.*
  I'm going to go for a jog in the park.

Life in France

LEISURE TIME

Le sport

CULTURAL TIPS

When the French are talking about rugby, you may hear a reference to *la troisième mi-temps*. This is literally the third half-time and refers to the celebrations after the match, which often involve heavy drinking.

Sports involving sliding or gliding movements such as skiing, surfing, snowboarding, skating and windsurfing are often referred to collectively in French as *les sports de glisse*.

When playing in a team or when in a particular sporting environment such as a club, the French will change to the informal *tu* form of the verb far more quickly than in other circumstances. This is particularly true in an all male group or an all female one.

France's victory in football's World Cup in 1998, with a team including players of different skin colours and racial origins, led to the concept of *le black-blanc-beur*, *beur* being the name given to young men born in France of North African immigrant parents. This combination was seen to be a winning formula and a recognition of the importance of racial harmony and integration.

In the 1960s, following the poor results of the French teams in the Olympics, young students showing potential in a particular sport were selected for training in specially created departments in certain schools throughout France. These departments were called *les sports-études* and they ran programmes that allowed for periods of training as well as the traditional school curriculum. Sports federations or professional clubs gave the complement of more specialised training needed. In 1996, these departments become known as *les sections sportives scolaires*. They still work in partnership with local clubs, continuing the tradition of cooperation between the State and voluntary and professional organisations.

🔊 ADVANCED USEFUL PHRASES

– *Vous préférez le ski de piste ou le ski de fond ?*
  Do you prefer downhill or cross-country skiing?
– *On peut louer des skis ?*
  Can we hire/rent skis?
– *Comment vous faites pour garder la ligne ?*
  How do you keep your figure?
– *J'aime bien faire du vélo, mais seulement sur les pistes cyclables.*
  I really like cycling, but only on cycle paths.
– *Je préfère être accompagnée par un moniteur.*
  I prefer to be accompanied by an instructor.
– *Vous faites du sport en semaine ?*
  Do you practise any sport during the week?
– *Vous faites beaucoup de ski l'hiver ?*
  Do you ski a lot in the winter?
– *Vous pratiquez le tennis ?*
  Do you play tennis?

LEISURE TIME

Le sport

 LANGUAGE TIPS

When talking about sport in French, it's useful to remember that *une partie* can be used when talking about different sports, although it is not translated by the same word in English. You can use *une partie*, for example, for a game of tennis, a football match or a round of golf. So you can say:

– *J'ai gagné la partie de tennis.*
I won the tennis game.

– *On a gagné la partie facilement.*
They won the match easily.

– *Je vais jouer une partie de golf.*
I'm going to play a round of golf.

Similarly, the word 'draw' in English in a sporting context can have different translations in French. So you would say:

– *Ils ont fait match nul.*
It ended in a draw.

– *Ils sont à égalité pour l'instant.*
It's a draw so far.

– *Ils ont fait deux partout.*
They drew two all.

– *Ils ont fait deuxième ex-æquo.*
They drew for second place.

Remember

When you hear French people talking about sport, you will hear several English words used, although the pronunciation will sometimes make it difficult for you to recognise them. Listen to a French football enthusiast talk about *un corner* and note how the pronunciation is not quite the same as in English!

In many sports, there is a mixture of French and English terms. French people discussing a football game will talk about *un penalty*, but also *un coup franc* and *un carton jaune* for a free kick and a yellow card. In tennis, you will hear *une balle de match* for match point, but that a player has won *un set*.

 LEARN MORE

You can find more examples of stating preferences in *L'éducation*, p.75.

You can refer to *Les rythmes de l'année*, p.29, for more examples of asking about people's habits.

LEISURE TIME

Le sport

Most famous

Two events dominate the sporting calendar in France: the French Open tennis tournament and Le Tour de France bicycle race.

The French Open is known by the name of the site where the tournament takes place in Paris, le stade Roland-Garros, named after a famous World War I French aviator. Roland-Garros runs over two weeks in late May and early June and is the largest and most famous clay-court tournament in the world. It is one of the four Grand Slam tournaments and the only one played on clay. The Frenchman Yannick Noah won Roland-Garros in 1983.

Le Tour de France is a gruelling bicycle race that is held annually. The first race was in 1903 and it has since become one of the world's top cycling events. The race takes place in July and lasts for three weeks with a finish on the Champs-Élysées. The route changes every year but always includes sections in the mountains and time trials. The overall winner gets to wear the famous yellow jersey. Every year millions of people line the route to watch the race.

Quiz

Circle the words that don't belong.

A. *les baskets, les skis, les chaussures de marche, les pantalons*

B. *un set, un corner, un ace, une raquette*

C. *le judo, le rugby, le football, le tennis*

D. *un short, un béret, un tee-shirt, un maillot*

E. *nager, surfer, plonger, grimper*

Answers: A. *les pantalons* (*les pantalons* are not worn on the feet), B. *un corner* (*un corner* is in football, not tennis), C. *le judo* (the others are ball sports), D. *un béret* (you don't wear a béret for a sporting activity), E. *grimper* (the others are water sports).

KEY POINTS

Le sport...

- in France means walks and longer hikes are popular.
- usually includes time spent skiing in the winter.
- has meant lasting popularity for key French sports personalities.
- is an element in the grading of school-leaving exams.
- includes two important sporting events: Le Tour de France and Roland-Garros.

Life in France

LEISURE TIME
Les vacances

Les vacances

WHAT TO EXPECT

Talk about the N7 to older French people and they will respond with nostalgic memories of their childhood holidays. The N7 was the longest *route nationale* in France, linking Paris to Menton, nearly a thousand kilometres away at the furthest extremity of the Côte d'Azur. It was the road to the sea and the sunshine of the South and nicknamed *la route des vacances*. Books were written about it and Charles Trenet famously sang about it.

Today, the summer traffic jams of the N7 have been replaced by those on the motorways: the A6 from Paris, and then, from Lyon on, the A7, known as *les autoroutes du soleil*. They are more practical routes to the south, but not as romantic. Their path does not meander through the centre of villages allowing for gastronomic stops on the way and there aren't the famous N7 kilometre markers, other, that is, than the replicas made of nougat sold in the large Montélimar service station on the A7. However, their purpose is the same: to allow for an escape from Paris and the reward of time at the seaside.

THE VAST MAJORITY OF FRENCH PEOPLE VACATION IN FRANCE.

CULTURAL TIPS

Many shops in France close for two to four weeks in July or August. In cities such as Paris, it can sometimes be necessary to walk further than usual to find a *boulangerie* or a *charcuterie* during these months. Shops re-open by the last week of August to be ready for the busy *rentrée* period when activities start up again after the summer break. Notices on shop doors give the dates they are closed for these *congés annuels*, or annual vacations.

Once a year, for their annual holiday, French employees can obtain a reduction of 25% on a round trip rail journey. The French railways supply a form that must be signed by the employer for the reduction to be granted.

The vast majority of French people vacation in France. They give the great variety of France's many regions as the reason for this. Another explanation is their preference for French cuisine!

Life in France

LEISURE TIME
Les vacances

Sometimes it can seem as if all of France is moving down to the South in July and August. In fact, although the predictable sun and the vibrancy of the Mediterranean coast continue to attract crowds, the French are also great lovers of the countryside. *Se mettre au vert*, to go to the country, is the ardent desire of many French people in the summer months. They rush off to their family homes in the country, rent holiday cottages and pitch their tents in remote corners.

They often go as a family with grandparents, aunts and uncles and nephews and nieces. This is particularly true for people who have a family home in the country as well as their apartment in town. A house in the country allows for all the family to meet up. Shopping and cooking is shared and the children enjoy the company of their cousins. It combines the desire to get away from the city in the summer months with the importance the French accord to family.

CULTURAL TIPS

During the skiing season and the summer holiday periods, the roads are extremely busy, especially at the weekends. The media announce the number of kilometres of traffic jams and advise holidaymakers to defer their departure. This has little effect as most people are anxious to start their holidays immediately, and rented accommodation usually runs from Saturday to Saturday.

Some companies try to make the most of the marketing opportunity created when lots of people are blocked in their cars for several hours. They distribute free bottles of water, sweets or games for children at the tollgates of the busiest motorways.

French workers have a minimum of five weeks paid holiday a year plus public holidays.

IDIOMS
– *C'est la montagne qui accouche d'une souris* means something is a lot of fuss for nothing.
– *Ce n'est pas la mer à boire* means it's no big deal.
– *Avoir les doigts de pied en éventail* means to have one's feet up.
– *Avoir des valises sous les yeux* is to have bags under one's eyes.

LEISURE TIME
Les vacances

Summer vacations are now shorter than in the past, however, leaving time for breaks at other moments in the year. A week skiing in the winter is a preferred option, although it also starts and finishes with traffic jams and often the need to use chains on the tyres to negotiate the last kilometres to the ski stations. However, once there, the French can indulge in one of their favourite sports and enjoy *raclette* and *fondue*, the traditional dishes essential on any skiing holiday.

A few long weekends, particularly in May when there are several public holidays, help to bridge the gap between skiing and *les grands départs* of the summer months. A recent trend for these early short holidays is to take a city break in a European capital or a few lazy days on a beach in Morocco or Tunisia. However, for most French people, it will still be those daunting traffic jams on the roads heading south that signal the start of the real holidays.

🔊 KEYWORDS

une valise	suitcase
le coffre de la voiture	car boot/trunk
un maillot de bain	swimming costume/swimsuit
une robe d'été	summer dress
au bord de la mer	at the seaside
à la campagne	in the country
à la montagne	in the mountains
un long week-end	long weekend
une quinzaine	fortnight/two weeks
les vacances	holidays
réserver	to book
camper	to camp
louer	to rent
se reposer	to rest
se détendre	to relax
prendre un bol d'air	to get a breath of fresh air
faire un tour	to tour
visiter	to visit

Life in France

LEISURE TIME
Les vacances

CULTURAL TIPS

Traditionally, Parisians and other city dwellers consider it impossible to stay in the cities during the hot summer months. This results in many cities being emptied of their normal residents, particularly during August. Traffic is lighter, car parking is often free and public transport is less crowded. It can be a great time to visit major cities, although you may feel surrounded by other tourists rather than by French people.

French people usually talk about *une quinzaine de jours* or 15 days when talking about a two-week holiday period. There are no extra days involved. Similarly they will refer to *une huitaine de jours* when talking about a one-week vacation.

HISTORY AND TRADITIONS

Les colonies de vacances, holiday camps, were and still are an institution in France. They were first established so that children from the working classes in the cities, who were often in poor health and suffering from tuberculosis, could benefit from the countryside, eat well and put on weight.

After the Second World War, trained instructors gradually replaced supervisors in the holiday camps. The instructors, or *moniteurs*, encouraged a playful approach, putting the focus on active participation. Parents came to see the holiday camps as a complement to the more traditional educational methods used during the school year.

🔊 USEFUL PHRASES

— *Quand est-ce que vous partez en vacances ?*
When are you going on holiday?
— *Où est-ce que vous partez ?*
Where are you going?
— *Vous partez combien de temps ?*
How long are you going for?
— *Vous allez au bord de la mer ?*
Are you going to the seaside?
— *Vous y allez en voiture ?*
Are you going by car?
— *Vous partez au mois d'août ?*
Are you going away in August?
— *Nous allons faire un tour en Bretagne.*
We're going touring in Brittany.
— *Je préfère prendre quelques jours en septembre.*
I prefer to take a few days in September.

Life in France

LEISURE TIME

Les vacances

 *Remember*

Holidays or vacations can have several different names in French depending on their nature and length.

A short holiday over a weekend with an extra day added will be called *un long week-end*. If it is extended further because the Tuesday or Thursday is a public holiday, it will be called *un pont*, the intervening day making literally a bridge with the public holiday. School holidays are *les vacances scolaires* and the main summer school holidays are called *les grandes vacances*.

Days taken off work may be called *des jours de congés* or *des jours de RTT* depending upon whether the leave is part of a person's paid holiday entitlement or compensatory time off. The latter is a result of the introduction of the 35-hour week (*réduction du temps de travail*) following which the hours worked up to 39 hours could be cumulated and taken as days off. The annual summer leave for employees is called *les congés annuels*.

YOU WILL HEAR

— *On prend la voiture. C'est plus simple.*
  We're going by car. It's easier.
— *Nous allons en Corse cette année.*
  We're going to Corsica this year.
— *Nous avons loué un gîte en Provence pour un mois.*
  We've rented a holiday cottage in Provence for a month.
— *Mes enfants adorent la mer.*
  My children love the seaside.
— *On prend trois semaines en juillet.*
  We're taking three weeks off in July.
— *Nous allons camper en Ardèche.*
  We're going camping in the Ardèche.
— *Nous partirons plus tard.*
  We'll go away later.
— *Nous allons nous reposer un peu.*
  We're going to rest a bit.

Gradually, children from the growing middle classes also began to spend part of the long summer school holidays in *les colos*, as they became known affectionately. As more mothers joined the work force, it became a practical way of giving children a safe and stimulating environment during the summer months when paid annual leave was shorter than the school holidays.

The heyday of *les colos* was in the 1960s. Since then, they have had to compete increasingly with foreign language courses and coaching in a variety of sports as parents decided their children needed to acquire added skills. For many French people, however, *les colos* remain a precious childhood experience.

Life in France

LEISURE TIME

Les vacances

Most famous

One of the most talked-about beaches in France in the summer is surprisingly in Paris. The operation Paris-Plages started in 2002 and has continued every summer since. Although most Parisians prefer to leave the capital during the hot summer months, not everyone is able to. So the Mayor of Paris, Bertrand Delanoë, decided it was time to bring the beaches to the capital.

From the middle of July, for four weeks, the roadways along the banks of the Seine are blocked and artificial beaches are created. Tons of sand, deck chairs and even palm trees are placed on the riverbanks, and millions of city dwellers and tourists enjoy relaxing on these beaches with the possibility of a dip in the specially installed floating swimming pool.

Towards the end of August, the sand is removed and the roads given back to the cars in time for the return of the Parisians who did leave the city.

LANGUAGE TIPS

If you telephone a French company and wish to speak to a specific person, you may be told the person is absent. When this is simply a temporary absence, you will hear:

– *Madame Caré n'est pas à son bureau.*
Mrs Caré is not at her desk.

– *Madame Robert ne travaille pas les mercredis.*
Mrs Robert doesn't work on Wednesdays.

– *Monsieur Perols est en rendez-vous à l'extérieur.*
Mr Perols is out of the office.

If the absence is because the person is on vacation, you may hear:
– *Madame Caré est en congé jusqu'au 17 aôut.*
Mrs Caré is on leave until August 17th.

Occasionally you may hear:
– *Madame Robert est en congé de maternité.*
Mrs Robert is on maternity leave.

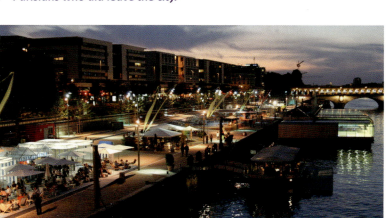

LEARN MORE

For further examples of asking questions, you can refer to *Les repas*, p.8.

You can find other examples of asking when activities take place in *L'emploi du temps*, p.22.

LEISURE TIME

Les vacances

Quiz

Fill in the blanks using the verbs below.
aimer, être, passer, quitter, louer, prendre.

A. Vous _____ la ville cet été ?

B. Vous _____ le train ?

C. Nous _____ une maison à la campagne.

D. Jean _____ en congé en ce moment.

E. Je _____ mes vacances en famille.

F. Les enfants n' _____ pas la montagne.

Answers: A. quittez, B. prenez, C. louons, D. est, E. passe, F. aiment.

🔊 ADVANCED USEFUL PHRASES

– *Vous mettez combien de temps pour faire le voyage ?*
  How long does the journey take?
– *Vous essayez d'éviter les vacances scolaires ?*
  Do you try to avoid the school holidays?
– *Est-ce que vous partez quelquefois à l'étranger ?*
  Do you go abroad sometimes?
– *Vous prenez beaucoup de petites vacances dans le courant de l'année ?*
  Do you take a lot of short breaks during the year?
– *Est-ce que les enfants vont partir avec vous ?*
  Are the children going away with you?
– *Vous ne craignez pas les embouteillages ?*
  Aren't you worried about the traffic jams?
– *Ça fait combien de kilomètres jusqu'à Nice ?*
  How many kilometres are there to Nice?
– *Vous voyagez les week-ends ou en semaine ?*
  Do you travel at the weekends or during the week?

KEY POINTS

Les vacances...

- mean many shops close for a period in July or August.
- are often spent with the extended family.
- mean many French people travel south during July and August.
- are the reason for many weekend traffic jams.
- include five weeks of annual paid leave.

Life in France

LEISURE TIME

As they say in French

- « Le rite bien français des vacances au bord de la mer constitue un voyage initiatique . »
  Michel Tournier

- « Je pensais que les vacances me videraient la tête. Mais non, les vacances, ça ne vide qu'une chose : le porte-monnaie. »
  Jean-Philippe Blondel

- « Chaque minute en Amazonie, on déboise l'équivalent de 60 terrains de football. C'est un peu idiot, il n'y aura jamais assez de joueurs. »
  Philippe Geluck

- « Chaque cycliste, même débutant, sait qu'à un moment ou un autre de sa vie il aura rendez-vous avec une portière de voiture. »
  Paul Fournel

- « Je n'ai rien contre les étrangers. Le problème, c'est que d'une part, ils parlent pas français pour la plupart. Et selon le pays où on va, ils parlent pas le même étranger. »
  Coluche

Life in France

LIFESTYLE

Le logement

Le logement

WHAT TO EXPECT

From an impressive, spacious apartment in a traditional Haussmannian building on one of Paris's main avenues to a miniscule *chambre de bonne*, or maid's room, under the rafters, the range of property for rent or purchase in France's capital city is enormous. However, there will be one common characteristic: it will be expensive.

The demand for apartments is considerable, particularly intra-muros in one of Paris's 20 *arrondissements*. Large apartments are difficult to find, especially on the average budget, so many people have to make do with small apartments, often on the upper floors of older buildings that don't have lifts or elevators. Extra square metres and the presence of a lift are an important factor in the rent or purchase price of an apartment.

Whether in Paris or other cities in France, the choice will be between an apartment in an older building, described familiarly as *dans l'ancien*, or in a modern block, *dans le neuf*. Traditional buildings will have the advantage of high ceilings, sometimes with the narrowly spaced beams characteristic of *les plafonds à la française*, parquet floors, vast fireplaces and French windows.

CULTURAL TIPS

The general upkeep, quality of construction and appearance of an apartment building is called *le standing*. If luxury apartments are described, they will be said to be *de grand standing*.

The suburbs of French cities, *les banlieues*, are, contrary to those in many English-speaking countries, often the most deprived areas of a city. They are generally associated with economic and social problems including, in some cases, violence and drugs. The connotations are comparable with those of the term 'inner city' in English.

Life in France

LIFESTYLE
Le logement

However, kitchens and bathrooms may be old-fashioned or very basic. Integrated kitchens in France are relatively recent, and it was common to purchase an apartment and find that all the kitchen cupboards had been removed. It is still wise to check on what is included when purchasing. Newer apartment buildings will, on the contrary, generally have modern kitchens and bathrooms. They will also often have the advantage of a balcony and a parking space, both of considerable value in crowded city centres.

French people, particularly young couples, wishing to buy an apartment or house may find it difficult. Property is expensive and loans are not easy to obtain. In addition to the purchase price, there are high taxes and legal fees.

As a result, France has one of the lowest home ownership rates in Europe. While having a house built can be a less expensive option, the cost of land is also high. Many small towns or larger villages sell parcels of land inexpensively to housing developers in the hope that this cheaper housing will encourage families to move into their district and consequently help local schools and shops.

IDIOMS
– *C'est la maison du bon Dieu* means their house is always open.
– *Faites comme chez vous* means make yourself at home.
– *C'est une vraie concierge* means she's a real gossip.
– *Renvoyer l'ascenseur* means to return a favour.

KEYWORDS

un appartement	flat/apartment
un studio	studio flat
un immeuble	block of flats/apartment building
une maison	house
une villa	villa, detached house
un terrain	plot (of land), land
un garage	garage
un balcon	balcony
une terrasse	terrace/patio
une véranda	veranda
un ascenseur	lift/elevator
un étage	floor/storey
les commodités	facilities
le centre-ville	town centre/downtown
la banlieue	suburbs
louer	to rent
acheter	to buy
vendre	to sell

THE DEMAND FOR APARTMENTS IS CONSIDERABLE, PARTICULARLY INTRA-MUROS IN ONE OF PARIS'S 20 *ARRONDISSEMENTS*.

Life in France

LIFESTYLE

Le logement

To help those most in need, administrative districts of a certain size that are part of an urban centre must build a percentage of subsidised rented accommodation. These can be pleasant buildings in small towns but are often in undesirable suburbs in larger cities. Waiting lists can be very long, meaning that many families can remain in inadequate or run-down accommodation for several years.

Finding rented accommodation at a reasonable price in country areas or small towns is generally easier. Some French families opt for what they consider to be a more favourable environment for their children, despite lengthy commutes to their place of work. But for those who enjoy big-city life or who choose to work in the popular sunny regions of the South of France, it is often a question of ensuring, as far as apartments are concerned, that small is beautiful.

CULTURAL TIPS

When the French talk about the apartment building where they live, you will hear them refer to *le syndic* or *la régie*. *Le syndic* is the agency mandated by the owners in *une copropriété* (an apartment building or a condominium in co-ownership) to oversee the running and maintenance of the building. *La régie immobilière* is an agency that acts as an intermediary between an owner and a tenant. Sometimes different departments of the same agency cover both these roles.

You may see a note in the lift in a French apartment building explaining that there will be a party in a particular apartment and apologising beforehand for any noise. Usually residents are not supposed to make noise that can disturb other residents between ten in the evening and seven in the morning. However, there is a degree of tolerance for occasional events, particularly if there is a prior apology!

FINDING RENTED ACCOMMODATION AT A REASONABLE PRICE IN COUNTRY AREAS OR SMALL TOWNS IS GENERALLY EASIER.

Life in France

LIFESTYLE
Le logement

HISTORY AND TRADITIONS

City-dwellers in France have traditionally lived in apartment buildings in city centres. This is still generally true today. Although some people have moved out to smaller towns nearby to escape from the noise and bustle, the cost of commuting causes many to stay. This means that city centres remain busy and lively even in the evenings, and that the demand for apartments, whether for rent or purchase, is great. As a result, they are increasingly expensive.

Apartments used to be classed, particularly in advertisements, as an F1, F2, F3 and so on, the F standing for *fonction*. This was the indication of the number of rooms, excluding the kitchen and bathroom, so an F2 was a two-room apartment. Nowadays, the same classification is used but is usually a T, standing for *type*, rather than an F.

ALTHOUGH SOME PEOPLE HAVE MOVED OUT TO SMALLER TOWNS NEARBY TO ESCAPE FROM THE NOISE AND BUSTLE, THE COST OF COMMUTING CAUSES MANY TO STAY.

🔊 USEFUL PHRASES

– *Vous habitez en appartement ?*
 Do you live in an apartment?
– *Vous êtes en centre-ville ?*
 Are you in the town centre?
– *Vous êtes à quel étage ?*
 What floor/storey are you on?
– *Vous avez un très bel appartement.*
 You have a lovely apartment.
– *C'est un joli immeuble ancien.*
 It's a lovely old apartment building.
– *Le balcon est très agréable.*
 The balcony is very pleasant.
– *Il y a un code pour entrer ?*
 Is there a code to come in?
– *La vue est magnifique.*
 The view is wonderful.

Life in France

LIFESTYLE

Le logement

The price of an apartment in France is traditionally based on the price per square metre in that particular area of the town or city. A potential buyer will take into consideration this average price and will multiply it by the number of square metres of the apartment for sale. There may be slight variations in the price, depending on the condition of the apartment or a particular feature. The price per square metre can vary considerably between a district considered desirable and a less popular one. The price per square metre in most districts of Paris is the highest in the country.

CULTURAL TIPS

Most French apartment buildings have a security system. This is either an access code, called *un Digicode*, which is entered on a small keyboard at the main entrance door that opens an electronic lock, or *un interphone*, an entry phone that rings the person you are visiting.

Before putting an apartment on the market, the owner is obliged by law, *la loi Carrez*, to have the surface area measured by a specialist so that the number of square metres indicated is accurate. This measurement, which doesn't include garages or cellars, must be included on all documents dealing with the sale. This law doesn't apply to houses.

In France, information on properties for sale can be found at an estate agency, called *une agence immobilière*, or at the notary's. The first part of a sale, *le compromis de vente* or preliminary sales agreement, can be drawn up and signed in the presence of either an agent or a notary, but the final act of sale must be established by *un notaire*.

A council flat or public housing unit for people with lower incomes is known as *un HLM*, standing for *une habitation à loyer modéré*, or rent-controlled housing.

Tenants in rented accommodation cannot be evicted in France between November and mid-March.

YOU WILL HEAR

— J'habite au deuxième.
I live on the second floor/storey.
— Je vais vous donner le code d'entrée.
I'll give you the entrance code.
— J'ai un grand appartement de cent mètres carrés.
I have a big apartment that's 100 square metres.
— J'ai un loyer très élevé.
I have a very high rent.
— J'habite à trente kilomètres de la ville.
I live 30 kilometres from town.
— Je cherche à acheter une maison.
I would like to buy a house.
— Je vais déménager dans une ville moins chère.
I'm going to move to a less expensive town.
— J'ai un tout petit appartement, mais c'est très bien situé.
I have a very small apartment, but it's very well located.

Life in France

LIFESTYLE

Le logement

🔊 LANGUAGE TIPS

Before entering into a conversation about housing, it is important to understand what the French consider to be positive features in an apartment. By understanding this, you can be sure to ask the relevant questions or give appropriate compliments.

For an apartment, spaciousness, light, windows on opposite walls allowing a breeze in the summer and the direction the apartment faces are all important. You can say:

– *Votre appartement est très lumineux et spacieux.*
Your apartment is very light and spacious.

– *C'est un avantage d'avoir un appartement traversant.*
It's an advantage to have an apartment where you can create a breeze.

– *C'est bien d'être orienté vers l'ouest. Le soleil en fin de journée est agréable.*
It's good to face west. It's pleasant to have the sun at the end of the day.

🔊 *Remember*

Avoid using the term *concierge* when referring to the person who sees to the cleaning and daily running of an apartment building.

For many years, apartment buildings, particularly in Paris, had a very small apartment near the main entrance called *la loge* where *la concierge* lived. This person was responsible for distributing the mail, keeping the entrance and staircase clean and ensuring unwanted persons didn't enter the building. The stereotypical *concierge* was considered to be a bit of a busybody and a gossip. Since the term became demeaning, this person is now called *la gardienne* or *le gardien d'immeuble*.

🔊 ADVANCED USEFUL PHRASES

– *Votre maison a été construite en quelle année ?*
  What year was your house built?
– *C'est pratique d'être si près d'une station de métro.*
  It's convenient to be so close to an underground/subway station.
– *Ça doit être difficile de trouver un appartement comme celui-ci.*
  It must be difficult to find an apartment like this one.
– *Vous avez dû faire beaucoup de travaux dans l'appartement.*
  You must have done a lot of work on the apartment.
– *Vous devez apprécier d'être au dernier étage.*
  You must appreciate being on the top floor/storey.
– *Est-ce que vous allez faire construire une maison plutôt que d'en acheter ?*
  Are you going to have a house built rather than buy one?
– *Nous avons acheté une maison et l'avons rénovée peu à peu.*
  We bought a house and have renovated it bit by bit.
– *Nous aimerions trouver une petite maison dans le Sud.*
  We'd like to find a small house in the South.

🐦 LEARN MORE

You can find other examples of asking for information in *Les sorties*, p.45.

Further examples of people describing an aspect of their lives can be found in *L'emploi du temps*, p.22.

Life in France

LIFESTYLE
Le logement

Most famous

A French film called TANGUY, released in 2001, was a black comedy depicting a young man of 28 who stubbornly refused to move out of his parents' comfortable home despite all their efforts to persuade him to do so. The film was extremely popular and the name 'Tanguy' became synonymous with young adults who did not wish to leave the family nest.

The economic situation of many young people has since changed dramatically. The difficulty of finding a job following the successive financial crises which started in 2008 means that many young people now continue to live with their parents out of necessity rather than choice. Even adults who have lived independently for a period of years are sometimes obliged to return to live with their parents while looking for a job or following a divorce.

Quiz

Are the following statements true or false?

A. The surface area, in square metres, influences the price of an apartment.
☐ True ☐ False

B. Most French apartments have parquet flooring.
☐ True ☐ False

C. Few people live in city centres in France.
☐ True ☐ False

D. A *concierge* is now usually called *un gardien d'immeuble*.
☐ True ☐ False

E. Apartment buildings generally have a security system at the entrance door.
☐ True ☐ False

F. A notary is necessary when signing the preliminary sales agreement on any property purchase.
☐ True ☐ False

Answers: A. True, B. False, C. False, D. True, E. True, F. False.

KEY POINTS

Le logement...

- in big cities is generally more expensive in the town centre than in the suburbs.
- in country regions and small towns is generally in individual houses.
- is expensive, meaning that the percentage of homeowners in France is below the European average.
- incurs high additional costs when purchasing.
- is a difficult problem and there are long waiting lists for subsidised housing.

LIFESTYLE

L'éducation

L'éducation

WHAT TO EXPECT

French schoolchildren will start nursery school, *la maternelle*, at the age of three and will study philosophy in their final year at secondary school. In between, they will have followed the teaching programme established by the Ministry of Education. It is the same for schoolchildren throughout France, as are the textbooks. This doesn't mean, though, that French children are expected to think alike. They are encouraged to express their opinions, taught how to debate and formally argue a viewpoint in a dissertation. It is not surprising that the French are known for their love of argument and discussion.

French children experience a radical change between nursery school and the years that follow. Nursery schools encourage discovery through play and have varied activities aimed at stimulating artistic development and autonomy as well as initiating children in reading and writing skills. France is a leader in Europe in nursery school education with almost all three-year-olds attending, as well as many two-year-olds. Stand in front of the school gates of any *maternelle* and you will be surprised at the number of very young children.

UNIVERSITIES IN FRANCE DO NOT HAVE A SELECTION PROCESS OTHER THAN *LE BACCALAURÉAT* QUALIFICATION.

CULTURAL TIPS

Schooling in France is obligatory from six to sixteen.

Pupils must purchase their own textbooks. To reduce costs, parent associations purchase used textbooks from families at the end of the school year and then sell them at a reduced price to the following year's students. All bookshops will also have displays of the listed books.

Pupils are given a list of supplies, *les fournitures scolaires*, that they will need for the school year. The list covers items such as pens, paper, folders, a calculator and compass. Most large stores will have aisles full of these products in August and there are always large crowds in the final days before the school year starts, *la rentrée*.

Life in France 75

LIFESTYLE

L'éducation

CULTURAL TIPS

At the age of 15 or 16, children take an examination known as *le brevet des collèges*. This is a national examination that is no longer considered to be very important, other than for children who do not continue their schooling beyond this age.

The final school-leaving examination, *le baccalauréat*, is very important in France. Students who pass the exam can enroll at a university. On a CV or résumé, when the word *bac* is followed by a plus sign and a number, this shows the number of years of formal study since obtaining the *bac*. A French person will say for instance, *"J'ai bac plus trois,"* or write *bac+3*. These abbreviations are often used in job advertisements.

Universities in France do not have a selection process other than *le baccalauréat* qualification. First-year courses are often crowded with lectures given to several hundred students at a time in large lecture halls. Many students fail the first-year exams and the dropout and failure rates continue to be high at the end of each year.

In primary school, between the ages of six and ten or eleven, life becomes much harder. School days are long, programmes are heavy, homework is introduced and results become a high priority. The typical child will be weighed down by a heavy school bag for the rest of his school career. It is from this age that children become instilled with the importance of *la moyenne*, their mark or grade averaged over all subjects. Depending upon this mark, they will be allowed to progress to the next year or not. Finally, they will need to obtain a score of 10 or more out of 20 in the *baccalauréat* examination that is essential for university entrance and further studies.

LIFESTYLE

L'éducation

Once children move to secondary school, *le collège* at 11 and *le lycée* at 15 or 16, teaching and supervision are clearly separated. Teachers teach and administrative staff see to everything else, including schedules, attendance and discipline issues. There will also be a difference between teachers. A teacher with a CAPES qualification, *un professeur certifié*, will teach more hours than *un professeur agrégé* who has passed the prestigious *agrégation* examination. The latter will also have the choice of classes and a higher salary.

In their final two years of schooling, *la première* and *la terminale*, French children will prepare for the *baccalauréat* examination which has several options. The *baccalauréat scientifique*, known as *le bac S*, is often chosen, even when it is not the preferred subject matter, as it is seen to be the most demanding and therefore the most valuable. Suprisingly, the *bac* that is taken does not necessarily relate to the subject the student goes on to study at a university. A student with a *bac S* may go on to study law, or a student with a literary *bac* may choose to study economics or even medicine.

SCHOOL DAYS ARE LONG, PROGRAMMES ARE HEAVY, HOMEWORK IS INTRODUCED AND RESULTS BECOME A HIGH PRIORITY.

🔊 KEYWORDS

la crèche	day nursery
l'école maternelle	nursery school
l'école primaire	primary/elementary school
le collège	secondary school/junior high school
le lycée	secondary school/high school
la cour de récréation	playground/schoolyard
un élève	pupil, student
un étudiant	student
un professeur	teacher, lecturer/instructor, professor
une salle de classe	classroom
un amphithéâtre	lecture hall/theater
un cours magistral	lecture
un bulletin scolaire	school report
une colle	detention
le brevet des collèges	exam taken at age 16
le baccalauréat	school-leaving examination
un diplôme	diploma, certificate, degree
une licence	(bachelor's) degree

Life in France

LIFESTYLE

L'éducation

Anyone who has passed the *baccalauréat* can enroll at a university, so student numbers are high and sometimes lectures have to be relayed for those who have not been able to find a place in the lecture hall. Many students will prefer alternative options such as the BTS or *brevet de technicien supérieur*. These courses have a more practical bias and are generally well-considered by employers. Gifted students will opt to follow preparatory classes and aim to enter one of the *grandes écoles*. Whatever the option, it will have been a long and demanding journey from the playful days of *la maternelle*.

CULTURAL TIPS

Throughout their schooling, children with poor results or learning difficulties can be required to repeat a year. This practice is known as *le redoublement*. It used to be extremely common, with many children repeating a year at least once in their school career. It is now more controversial and fewer children are affected.

Pupils that have good results will often prefer to aim for *les grandes écoles*. These are prestigious, higher-education institutes with competitive entrance examinations. In order to have a chance of being accepted, a student must study an extra two years after *le baccalauréat* in special sections called *les classes préparatoires*, often referred to as *les prépas*. These are intensive classes with demanding programmes that can only be followed in certain reputed *lycées*.

IDIOMS

- *Faire l'école buissonnière* is to play truant.
- *Être à bonne école* is to be in good hands.
- *On n'apprend pas à un vieux singe à faire des grimaces* means you don't teach your grandmother to suck eggs/ teach someone something they already know.
- *Jouer dans la cour des grands* is to play in the major league or with the big boys.

USEFUL PHRASES

- *Tu es en quelle année ?*
  What year are you in?
- *Tu travailles bien à l'école ?*
  Do you work hard at school?
- *Tu as beaucoup de devoirs ?*
  Do you have a lot of homework?
- *Tu passes ton bac cette année ?*
  Are you taking the *baccalauréat* exam this year?
- *Vous êtes professeur au collège ?*
  Are you a teacher in the secondary school?
- *Il y a combien d'enfants dans la classe de CP ?*
  How many children are there in the first-year class in the primary school?
- *Votre fille a commencé l'école maternelle à quel âge ?*
  How old was your daughter when she started nursery school?
- *Est-ce que votre fils a eu son bac ?*
  Did your son pass his *baccalauréat*?

Life in France

LIFESTYLE

L'éducation

 *Remember*

There are some expressions in French when talking about education that can easily trip you up.

To pass an exam in French is *réussir un examen*. *Passer un examen* means simply to take an exam. And don't be surprised if a young person refers to *sécher l'école*. Literally translated, 'to dry school' may indeed seem odd, but it actually means to skive off or skip school.

Un pion can be translated by a pawn, as in chess. It is also the slang name given to *un surveillant*, the person, usually a university student, who helps maintain discipline and who supervises pupils when teachers are not present.

Don't forget that if a French person tells you he is a *professeur*, it doesn't necessarily mean he has a chair in a university. Any teacher in secondary or in higher education is known as *un professeur*.

HISTORY AND TRADITIONS

A nursery or primary school teacher used to be called *un instituteur*. When reading French novels or when visiting museums depicting local life, you will find many references to *l'instituteur*. His role was an important one. In many small villages there was only one class in the primary school and *l'instituteur* taught the children together. *L'instituteur* knew all the village children and was a point of reference because of his learning. It was always considered that there were three key male figures in a village: the priest *(le curé)*, the mayor *(le maire)* and *l'instituteur*.

The first *instituteurs* appeared during the French Revolution. Since the priests had been banished, illiteracy had become a real problem. The State, therefore, took over the traditional teaching role of the church and organised the training of teachers known as *les instituteurs*. Poorly paid and working without proper means, the life of an *instituteur* was not an easy one. Finally, in 1889, they became State employees. After the law of 1905 consolidated the separation of church and State, their status and pay gradually improved.

Since 1989, *les instituteurs*, traditionally trained in teacher training colleges, *les écoles normales*, are gradually being replaced by *les professeurs des écoles* who have a university degree. Since 2010, primary school teachers have been required to have a master's degree.

Although it is best to refer to a primary school teacher as *un professeur des écoles*, you will still hear French people talk about *l'instituteur*, frequently shortened to *l'instit*. Old habits die hard.

Life in France

LIFESTYLE

L'éducation

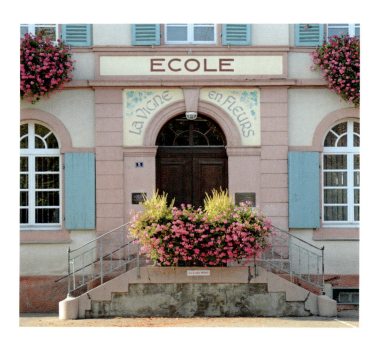

🔊 LANGUAGE TIPS

There are many abbreviations in the academic world, so it's best to know the most commonly used ones in advance.

In primary schools, the classes are referred to by their initials, so the first year, called *le cours préparatoire*, is known as *le CP*. The second and third years, *les cours élémentaires*, are referred to as *le CE1* and *le CE2*. The final two years, *les cours moyens*, are known as *le CM1* and *le CM2*.

In secondary schools, the teacher, *le professeur,* will be referred to as *le prof*. *Le conseiller principal d'éducation*, the person responsible for day-to-day issues concerning students, is known as *le CPE*, and, of course, the final year examination, *le baccalauréat*, is called *le bac*.

University is commonly referred to as *la fac*, an abbreviation of *la faculté*.

🔊 YOU WILL HEAR

— *Ma fille est en CP.*
    My daughter is in the first year at primary school.
— *Mon fils est en terminale.*
    My son is in the upper sixth form/12th grade.
— *Je suis en fac de médecine.*
    I'm at medical school.
— *Je fais une école de commerce.*
    I'm at business school.
— *Mon fils fait un doctorat.*
    My son is working towards his Ph.D.
— *Ma femme est prof au collège local.*
    My wife is a teacher at the local secondary/junior high school.
— *Je n'aime pas trop les maths.*
    I don't like maths much.
— *Je vais passer mon bac cette année.*
    I'm taking my school-leaving exam this year.

 **LEARN MORE**

For more examples of asking about future intentions, you can refer to *À la maison,* p.38.

You can refer to *Les repas*, p.8, for more examples of asking questions.

Life in France

LIFESTYLE
L'éducation

Most famous

The *Lycée Henri IV*, situated in the *Quartier Latin* in Paris, is one of the most highly regarded *lycées* in France. The school was first established in 1796 in a former abbey and its most famous symbol is the Clovis bell tower that dates from the Middle Ages. The school takes children from all over France and competition for places is fierce. It generally has a 100% success rate for the *baccalauréat* exam and prepares many students for *les grandes écoles*. Among former pupils are Guy de Maupassant and Jean-Paul Sartre.

L'École nationale d'administration, known as *l'ÉNA*, is one of the most prestigious higher-education institutions in France. Created by Général de Gaulle in 1945, it trains senior French and Francophone officials.

Its graduates are known as *les énarques*. They occupy top administrative positions and often move into senior industry positions or politics. The school's alumni include Jacques Chirac, François Hollande and many government ministers and industry leaders.

ADVANCED USEFUL PHRASES

– *Quelle est ta matière préférée ?*
  What's your favourite subject?
– *Tu as eu combien au bac ?*
  What mark/grade did you get in the *baccalauréat*?
– *Tu vas faire une prépa maintenant ?*
  Are you going to prepare for the entrance exams for *les grandes écoles* now?
– *Vous avez combien d'années d'études encore ?*
  How many more years of studying do you have?
– *Qu'est-ce que vous avez l'intention de faire par la suite ?*
  What do you intend to do afterwards?
– *Est-ce que vous allez faire un stage à l'étranger ?*
  Are you going to do a training period/internship abroad?
– *Vous allez continuer avec les études ?*
  Are you going to carry on with your studies?
– *Qu'est-ce que votre fille fait comme études ?*
  What is your daughter studying?

Quiz

Fill in the blanks using the word bank below.
matière, résultat, surveillant, bulletin, lycée, devoirs.

A. *J'étudie la philosophie au _____.*

B. *Ce soir j'ai beaucoup de _____.*

C. *Le français n'est pas ma _____ préférée.*

D. *Je travaille comme _____ pendant mes études.*

E. *J'attends le _____ du bac avec impatience.*

F. *Ma mère n'était pas contente avec mon _____ scolaire.*

Answers: A. lycée, B. devoirs, C. matière, D. surveillant, E. résultat, F. bulletin.

KEY POINTS

L'éducation...

- in France is based on a national curriculum.
- separates teaching and administrative functions in secondary schools.
- means many children go to nursery schools.
- gives great emphasis to the *baccalauréat* examination.
- has a number of prestigious higher-education institutions.

LIFESTYLE

Le travail

Le travail

WHAT TO EXPECT

If you wanted to discretely observe life in a French office, you might wish you were a fly on the wall, although in France you would have to be *une petite souris*, as the French seem to feel mice are more adequate in this role! What would you notice that might surprise you?

First of all, as people arrive in the morning, you would see that a certain amount of time is spent on greeting each other. There's no airy *"Bonjour!"* to everybody in the room. Whether it's the boss, the newest recruit or the lowest on the pay scale, everybody will greet each other individually. This can take the form of a handshake, a simple verbal greeting, or, depending on age and status, *une bise* or kiss on both cheeks. Only after having greeted everyone will people settle into their working routine.

CULTURAL TIPS

People who work shifts in factories are said to work *'les trois huits'*, that is, one of three eight-hour shifts. They will usually have to clock in, or *pointer*, when they arrive.

When French people talk about their work, they use a lot of slang. You will often hear people use the verb *bosser* instead of *travailler* for the verb to work, and they will refer to their company as *ma boîte* rather than *mon entreprise*. As with all slang expressions, it is important to become familiar with the most common terms but to refrain from using them yourself unless you're certain it is appropriate.

🔊 IDIOMS

– *Un travail de Romain* is a Herculean task.
– *C'est du beau travail !* means 'Nice work!'
– *L'inspecteur des travaux finis* is a humorous title given to someone who arrives when the work has been done.
– *Travailler comme une bête de somme* means to work like a Trojan/like a horse.

LIFESTYLE
Le travail

The first meeting of the morning may also hold its surprises for you. It will probably not start on time and although there may be an agenda, *un ordre du jour*, you might find it hard to believe as people appear to go back and forth from one point to another. The discussion on particular issues may even become heated, but remember lively debate is usually enjoyed in France.

At lunchtime, don't expect people to get out their sandwiches and eat at their desks. A proper break and something tempting to eat, either in the company canteen or in a local *café*, is considered essential, even if lunchtimes are not as long as they used to be. And although meetings often begin late, the start of the lunch break is generally fairly precise. Try calling a French company just after noon and you'll see!

🔊 KEYWORDS

un employeur	employer
un employé	employee
un ouvrier	worker
un salarié	salaried employee
un cadre	executive, manager
un dirigeant d'entreprise	company director, manager
un patron	boss, owner
le comptable	accountant
le secrétaire	secretary
l'accueil	reception
le bureau	office, desk
l'usine	factory
un rapport	report
le chômage	unemployment
une entreprise	firm, company
un syndicat	union
travailler	to work
être en réunion	to be in a meeting

LIFESTYLE

Le travail

CULTURAL TIPS

The boss in a company is *le patron* in French, but you may also hear him referred to as *le big boss*, *le chef*, or more pejoratively as *le singe*, the monkey.

In some French companies, employees receive what is known as *le treizième mois*, the 13th month. This is a bonus equivalent to an extra month's salary, usually paid at the year's end. It is part of the work contract, not an occasional bonus, and is used as an enticement to attract and keep staff. Certain companies even offer *le quatorzième mois*, but this is far more rare!

It is a legal requirement in France for every employee to have a work contract. Employees nearly always prefer to have permanent contracts as they can find it difficult to rent an apartment or obtain a bank loan without one. However, companies are often reluctant because of the complex rules in France when making people redundant or firing them. Many companies prefer therefore to issue short-term contracts, particularly in difficult economic times.

Finally, around six in the evening, most people will pack up and leave, not forgetting to say goodbye to their colleagues. Executives, *les cadres*, may stay on longer, as that is what is expected of them. Of course, if it's a Friday afternoon, there probably won't be many people in the office. The 35-hour working week means that Friday afternoons are no longer on many people's timetable. The motorways, though, will be busy even earlier in the afternoon than usual as people rush to their second homes in the countryside, or the sunnier South, for what they consider to be a well-deserved break from the world of *le travail*.

SOCIAL SECURITY CONTRIBUTIONS PAID BY EMPLOYEES AND EMPLOYERS ARE HIGH IN FRANCE.

🔊 USEFUL PHRASES

– *Où est-ce que vous travaillez ?*
  Where do you work?
– *Vous avez un travail à plein temps ?*
  Do you have a full-time job?
– *Vous aimez votre travail ?*
  Do you like your job?
– *Vous travaillez dans l'industrie ?*
  Do you work in the industrial sector?
– *Je travaille de chez moi.*
  I work from home.
– *Je suis médecin.*
  I'm a doctor.
– *Mon patron est très sympa.*
  My boss is very nice.
– *Je travaille dans une petite entreprise.*
  I work in a small company.

Life in France

LIFESTYLE

Le travail

HISTORY AND TRADITIONS

Until the early part of the 19th century, the working day in France was between 15 and 17 hours long. It was only in 1848 that the maximum number of hours worked in a day was limited to 12, but this limit didn't last very long with the pace of industrialisation, and there was frequent abuse.

In 1864, workers began to demand an eight-hour working day. Support was sought for this on an international scale and workers in several countries decided to make the 1st of May a day of general mobilization every year to pursue this claim. Not long after, the working day was reduced to 10 hours, and in 1906, Sunday was made a day of rest. Finally, in 1919, the length of the working day was fixed at eight hours, six days a week.

A huge strike, led by the *Front populaire* in 1936, brought a further reduction to 40 hours per week and introduced the practice of paid holidays, set at two weeks at the time.

🔊 YOU WILL HEAR

– *Je travaille dans un bureau en centre-ville.*
  I work in an office in the city centre/downtown.
– *Mon patron est expert-comptable.*
  My boss is a chartered/certified public accountant.
– *Désolé, mon bureau est submergé sous les dossiers.*
  I'm sorry, my desk is buried under files.
– *J'ai une entreprise de quinze personnes.*
  I have a company with 15 employees.
– *Qu'est-ce que vous faites comme travail ?*
  What do you do for a living?
– *Vous avez des collègues sympathiques ?*
  Are your colleagues nice?
– *Vous travaillez combien d'heures par semaine ?*
  How many hours a week do you work?
– *Vous avez créé votre société ?*
  Did you set up your company?

Life in France

LIFESTYLE

Le travail

CULTURAL TIPS

When there is a disagreement over dismissals or other issues in the workplace, an employee can make a complaint to an industrial tribunal, *les prud'hommes*. Employers follow strict procedures when letting an employee go, as they fear having to pay compensation should the employee have recourse to *les prud'hommes*.

Travailler au noir, to work without being declared by an employer is, of course, an offence. The expression can also be used to describe a moonlighting activity. In slang, moonlighting can also be called *travailler au black*.

Social security contributions paid by employees and employers are high in France. On average, they total about 64% of the gross salary, although this can vary depending on the salary and various reductions for low-paid workers.

Following a return to longer hours before and during the First World War, the post-war government reintroduced a 40-hour week but with the possibility of working extra hours which had to be paid at a higher rate. Gradually, more weeks of paid holiday were added, and in 1982, the working week was reduced to 39 hours and the number of weeks of paid holiday increased to five.

In 1998, Martine Aubry introduced the idea of a 35-hour working week. It became law in 1999 and came into force for larger companies in 2000 and for smaller ones in 2002. The following right-wing government introduced measures to make the law more flexible, but the 35-hour week is still in force for the moment.

IN 1998, MARTINE AUBRY INTRODUCED THE IDEA OF A 35-HOUR WORKING WEEK, WHICH IS STILL IN FORCE.

🔊 ADVANCED USEFUL PHRASES

– *Vous travaillez depuis longtemps dans cette entreprise ?*
   How long have you been working for this company?
– *Qu'est-ce que vous aimez dans votre travail ?*
   What do you like about your work?
– *Il y a combien de salariés dans votre entreprise ?*
   How many employees are there in your company?
– *C'est difficile de démarrer sa propre entreprise ?*
   Is it difficult to start your own company?
– *Je travaille dans le secteur bancaire.*
   I work in the banking sector.
– *J'ai créé ma propre entreprise il y a trois ans.*
   I started my own company three years ago.
– *Je suis souvent en tournée toute la journée.*
   I'm often on the road all day.
– *C'est un secteur en plein développement.*
   It's a sector that's really expanding.

Life in France

LIFESTYLE

Le travail

🔊 LANGUAGE TIPS

When talking to French people about their work, you will often hear them referring to *mon boulot* rather than *mon travail*. They may even talk about *mon job*, using the English word now commonly used in French. *Boulot* and *job* are not always completely interchangeable, though.

When talking about looking for work, either can be used, as in:
– *Je cherche un boulot plus près de chez moi.*
– *Je cherche un job plus près de chez moi.*
I'm looking for a job nearer home.

Or a French person could say:
– *Ce n'est pas mon job de faire ça.*
– *Ce n'est pas mon boulot de faire ça.*
It's not my job to do that.

However, in some circumstances a person would only use the word *boulot,* as in:
– *Quand je rentre du boulot, je suis crevé.*
When I get home from work, I'm worn out.

– *J'ai un boulot fou en ce moment.*
I'm up to my eyes in work at the moment.

You may also hear it said of someone:
– *Il est boulot, boulot.*
With him it's just work, work, work.

🔊 *Remember*

Certain words to do with work have more than one meaning. When French people refer to *le bureau*, they may be talking about the office where they work or specifically about their desk. Only the context will tell you which one.

The word *cadre* means an executive, and *un cadre supérieur* is a senior executive. However, *un cadre* can also be the frame of a painting, or more widely a framework, as in *dans le cadre de la réorganisation*. In other contexts, it can be a setting, as in a countryside setting, or even the space on a form, as in *Ne rien écrire dans ce cadre*, instructing you not to write in this space.

And remember that while *le patron* is, of course, the boss, the word can also mean a pattern as in a dress pattern!

🐦 LEARN MORE

You can find other examples of asking questions in *Les vacances*, p.59.

You can refer to *Le sport*, p.52, for other examples of describing what you do.

Life in France

LIFESTYLE

Le travail

Most famous

The world of work in France is famous for its acronyms. The most commonly used for talking about a company are *une TPE* for *une très petite entreprise*, a very small company, and *une PME*, *une petite et moyenne entreprise*, for small or medium-sized companies.

A company in France will either be *une SARL* or *une SA*. The first is *une société à responsabilité limitée*, a limited liability company, and the latter *une société anonyme*, a larger limited or public company.

Work contracts in France are of two kinds, *un CDD, un contrat à durée déterminée*, or fixed-term contract, and *un CDI, un contrat à durée indéterminée*, or permanent contract.

Le SMIC is the minimum wage, *le salaire minimum interprofessionnel de croissance*.

Le DRH is the *directeur de ressources humaines* and *le PDG* or *président-directeur général* is the CEO.

A famous, more recent addition is *la RTT*, standing for *la réduction du temps de travail*, which is vacation hours that can be accumulated since the controversial move to a 35-hour week.

Quiz

Match the first half of the sentence with its second half.

A. *En France, un contrat de travail...* 1. *de leurs droits.*
B. *Les salariés préfèrent s'arrêter...* 2. *se saluent.*
C. *En arrivant au bureau les gens...* 3. *un ordre du jour.*
D. *Un employeur doit déclarer...* 4. *est obligatoire.*
E. *Dans une réunion, il y a...* 5. *pour manger à midi.*
F. *Les Français ont conscience...* 6. *tous les salariés.*

Answers: A.4, B.5, C.2, D.6, E.3, F.1.

KEY POINTS

Le travail...

- in France is based on a 35-hour working week.
- is strictly regulated with complex rules.
- has many acronyms connected with it in daily use.
- incurs heavy employee and employer contributions.
- is associated with a strong sense of hierarchy.

Life in France

LIFESTYLE

La mode

La mode

WHAT TO EXPECT

When the British Queen Elizabeth II made an official visit to Paris in the 70s, a Parisian newspaper dedicated an entire page to discussing and illustrating how the Queen carried her handbag. This attention to detail is typical of the French approach to fashion, *la mode*. Fashion is a way of life in France. People care about the way they look and the image they project.

The French can dress up, but they are also masters of a casual chic. Casual means relaxed, but never untidy or shapeless. Tracksuits are worn in the gym, but not in the street. A pullover across the shoulders will have the sleeves tied in front just so.

A scarf will seem to fall just right to give an extra degree of elegance to a classic coat and a piece of costume jewellery will give, as the French say, a touch of *'fantaisie'* to a simple dress.

FASHION IS A WAY OF LIFE IN FRANCE.

CULTURAL TIPS

Coco Chanel suggested that everyone should look in the mirror before leaving the house and remove one item, such as a belt or a necklace, before going out.

In boutiques in France, shop assistants selling clothes or accessories will often show you how best to tie a scarf or stylishly adjust the clothes item you are purchasing.

In a perfume shop, *une parfumerie*, you can try perfumes and purchase cosmetics and skin care products. These shops are extremely busy around Mother's Day, Valentine's Day and during December as French people consider perfume to be an excellent gift.

Life in France

LIFESTYLE

La mode

This elegance is not limited to women. French men also have a certain style. The shirt collar will be adjusted at just the right angle, the scarf knotted casually but fashionably, and the shoes will be chosen to go with the overall look.

It is the simplicity of French elegance that is striking, and above all, the confidence with which the French wear their clothes. The sense of what looks right seems to be innate, and elegant men and women are not just the exception, as you will quickly notice if you sit at a pavement *café* in France and watch the passers-by. You will soon be convinced that the majority of French people you see have definitely looked in a mirror before leaving their home!

THE SENSE OF WHAT LOOKS RIGHT SEEMS TO BE INNATE.

CULTURAL TIPS

The French tend to dress more formally than in some countries. In a business context, men will wear suits, although ties are becoming less obligatory. Men and women may wear jeans to work in some companies, but they will usually be matched with a smart blouse or jacket. Shorts or sportswear are not usually acceptable in the workplace. In seaside resorts, restaurants will not accept swimwear, but smart shorts with a tidy top can be worn in all but the best restaurants. The French often express surprise at the lack of formality in dress of other nationalities, so it is always best when in France to err on the side of formality if in doubt.

When French people dress up for a special occasion, they say they are on their 31, *se mettre sur son trente-et-un*. The origin of this expression is probably the popular 19th century card game of the same name where to win you had to obtain 31 points, the last point being the most valuable and therefore the best. The verb *s'endimancher* also exists with its reference to Sunday.

Life in France

LIFESTYLE

La mode

French style is, of course, a source of national pride. French luxury goods are among the most reputed and successful in the world, whether it's clothes, accessories, perfume or cosmetics. Paris Fashion Week is always a highlight on the calendar and attracts comments — and more importantly, buyers — from all over the world. Tradition, know-how, hours of talented work and innovation combine to produce dramatic, artistic displays with eye-catching clothes that launch fashions around the globe.

Yet, it is the way the average French person seems to know how to put the few chosen articles in his or her wardrobe together that is truly impressive. The expression *la French touch* is used somewhat self-mockingly by the French themselves and with an accent considered to be charming by most foreigners. It is just this French touch which makes the French stand out as they make their way elegantly and confidently about their everyday business.

KEYWORDS

un look	look, image
le design	design
un créateur	designer
la coupe	cut
un foulard	scarf
un sac à main	handbag/purse
une ceinture	belt
les bijoux	jewellery
le parfum	scent/perfume
tendance	trendy
chic	smart, stylish
soigné	well-groomed, neat
s'habiller	to get dressed, wear
porter	to wear
mettre	to put on, wear
essayer	to try on
se maquiller	to put (one's) make-up on
se coiffer	to do one's hair

IDIOMS

- *Se faire coiffer au poteau* means to be pipped at the post, or narrowly defeated at the last moment.
- *Être au parfum* means to be in the know.
- *C'est un bijou* means it's a gem.
- *Avoir le chic pour faire quelque chose* means to have the knack of doing something.

Life in France

LIFESTYLE

La mode

CULTURAL TIPS

A blouse can be called *un corsage*, but this has become a little old-fashioned. It is now usually referred to as *un chemisier*, although this implies that it has buttons. You may hear a shop assistant propose *un petit haut*, a little top, to go with a skirt you are buying. Note that *une blouse* exists in French but it means an overall or smock; however, it is now sometimes used on shopping websites with the English meaning of blouse.

You may hear French people refer to *les fringues* when talking about fashion. This is simply the slang word for clothes.

If you want to try on an item of clothing before purchasing it, you need to ask for *la cabine d'essayage*.

HISTORY AND TRADITIONS

French fashion came to the fore in Europe during the reign of Louis XIV. French fashion journals already existed and had introduced the concept of changing fashions and the copying of fashions worn in the French court. Extravagant curled wigs were one of the more notable fashions of the period that spread from France to other European countries.

The French Revolution, with its rejection of an aristocratic lifestyle, broke the rules of dress of the time and introduced the idea of a more democratic approach to fashion.

France came to dominate the fashion world again in the late 19th and early 20th centuries with its concept of *la haute couture*. Some of the great fashion houses were created during this period, including Chanel. Live models were used for the first time and fashion shows were introduced. In the fashion press, the magazine ELLE was founded in 1945. VOGUE had already come to Europe in 1910.

USEFUL PHRASES

– *C'est très chic.*
  It's very stylish.
– *Est-ce que ça me va ?*
  Does it suit me?
– *Est-ce que ce sera une réunion très formelle ?*
  Will it be a very formal meeting?
– *Votre ensemble est très joli.*
  Your outfit is very pretty.
– *Je voudrais offrir du parfum à une amie.*
  I would like to buy some perfume for a friend.
– *C'est très à la mode.*
  It's very fashionable.
– *Je voudrais essayer cette robe, s'il vous plaît.*
  I'd like to try on this dress, please.
– *Vous auriez un foulard pour aller avec cette veste ?*
  Do you have a scarf to go with this jacket?

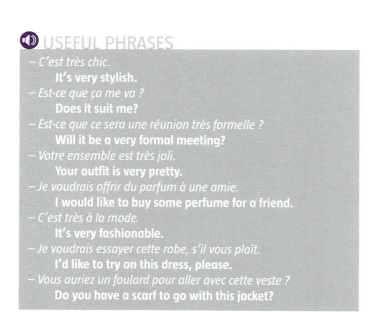

LIFESTYLE
La mode

During the Second World War, many fashion houses in Paris closed. But in 1947, the famous 'New Look' collection of Dior signalled the end of the austerity of the war years with a celebration of elegance and abundant fabrics and Paris again became the capital of high fashion. It was Yves Saint Laurent who brought high fashion to the mass market in the 1960s. He was followed by Cardin, Gaultier and Christian Lacroix.

Despite increasing competition, Paris Fashion Week, which takes place twice a year, is still the most eagerly awaited event on the fashion calendar.

FRANCE CAME TO DOMINATE THE FASHION WORLD AGAIN IN THE LATE 19TH AND EARLY 20TH CENTURY WITH ITS CONCEPT OF *LA HAUTE COUTURE*.

LOUIS VUITTON IS THE WORLD'S MOST VALUABLE LUXURY BRAND.

🔊 Remember

English words such as 'look' and 'design' don't have quite the same meaning when used in French. *Un look* in French has much more to do with building an image or a certain style, as in *soigner son look*, which means to cultivate one's image, or *changer de look*, meaning to change one's image. Amusingly, the verb *relooker* also exists, meaning to revamp something, and *se relooker* means to intentionally change one's image.

Similarly, *design* used as an adjective, as in *des meubles design*, is often the equivalent of 'designer' in English. In this case, designer furniture would suggest furniture that is modern, functional, well-constructed and probably expensive.

Remember, also, that *"Chic !"* when used as an exclamation has nothing to do with style but means "Great!"

🔊 YOU WILL HEAR

– *Ça vous va bien.*
    It really suits you.
– *C'est très tendance.*
    It's very trendy.
– *Elle est toujours très élégante.*
    She's always very elegant.
– *Il a complètement changé de look.*
    He's changed his image completely.
– *Il vous faut un bijou fantaisie pour aller avec cette robe.*
    You need a piece of costume jewellery to go with that dress.
– *Je vous parfume ?*
    Would you like to try some perfume?
– *Ils ont un intérieur très design.*
    They have a designer interior.
– *Il a beaucoup de goût.*
    He has good taste.

Life in France

LIFESTYLE

La mode

 LANGUAGE TIPS

You will need to deal with three verbs when talking about wearing clothes in French.

Mettre means 'to put on' but could also be translated by 'to wear' in certain contexts:
– *Mettez votre costume gris.*
Put your grey suit on.

– *Je ne sais pas quoi mettre.*
I don't know what to wear.

Habiller means 'to dress' and *s'habiller,* 'to dress oneself', but again both can sometimes be translated by 'to wear':
– *Habillez-vous chaudement.*
Dress warmly.

– *Comment vous habillez-vous pour le mariage ?*
What are you wearing for the wedding?

Porter usually means 'to wear' in the context of clothes:
– *Il porte toujours un chapeau.*
He always wears a hat.

Notice, however, the use of *porter* in the sense of something being fashionable:
– *Le gris se porte beaucoup cette année.*
Grey is very fashionable this year.

ADVANCED USEFUL PHRASES

– *Il faut que je me coiffe.*
I must do my hair.
– *Je ne sais pas comment m'habiller.*
I don't know what to wear.
– *Quel est le parfum que vous portez ?*
What perfume are you wearing?
– *Vous auriez un petit haut pour aller avec cette jupe ?*
Do you have a top to go with this skirt?
– *Merci pour votre cadeau. Vous avez beaucoup de goût.*
Thank you for your gift. You have very good taste.
– *Qu'est-ce que vous aimez comme parfum ?*
What perfume do you like?
– *C'est très tendance, mais je n'aime pas beaucoup la couleur.*
It's very trendy, but I don't like the colour very much.
– *Est-ce que vous pensez que les Français s'habillent bien ?*
Do you think the French dress well?

 **LEARN MORE**

For more examples of giving compliments, you can refer to *Le logement*, p.68.

You can find other examples of asking questions in *L'éducation*, p.75.

LIFESTYLE
La mode

Most famous

There are numerous famous companies with luxury brands in France. Hermès is one of the most successful. It was founded by Thierry Hermès, who set up as a maker of harnesses in 1837. His workshop soon became famous for the quality of its products. The shop moved to its present site in the Faubourg Saint-Honoré in 1880 and succeeding generations started to introduce other products, including leather saddles and bags. The famous Hermès scarves were introduced in 1937 and Grace Kelly was photographed carrying a Hermès handbag, which became known as *le sac Kelly*, adding to the renown of the brand.

Today, Hermès is world-famous for its products, which include scarves, bags, ties and perfumes.

Louis Vuitton, a division of LVMH, is another extremely successful brand. It was founded in Paris in 1854 by Louis Vuitton who introduced flat-top travelling trunks. The famous beige and brown stripe design was added in 1876. In 1987, the company merged with Moët et Chandon and Hennessey to form the world's most valuable luxury brand. Today, with a large range of travel bags and handbags, Louis Vuitton is one of the companies whose products are most often counterfeited.

Quiz

Fill in the blanks using the verbs below.
porter, essayer, aller, être, s'habiller, changer

A. *Votre robe _____ très chic.*
B. *Ce style ne se _____ plus.*
C. *Elle ne sait pas _____.*
D. *Est-ce que ça me _____ ?*
E. *Tu _____ de look tous les jours !*
F. *Vous voulez _____ ce pantalon avant de l'acheter?*

Answers: A. est, B. porte, C. s'habiller, D. va, E. changes, F. essayer.

KEY POINTS

La mode...

- is a key industry in France.
- seems to be an innate sense for many French people.
- is often a mixture of classic clothes and carefully chosen accessories.
- has a long history in France.
- is characterised by something known as *la French touch*.

Life in France

As they say in French

- « Si une femme est mal habillée, on remarque sa robe, mais si elle est impeccablement vêtue, c'est elle que l'on remarque. »
  Coco Chanel

- « Il n'a que dans le dictionnaire que réussite vient avant travail. »
  Pierre Fornerod

- « Si votre femme a envie d'habiter un appartement plus cher, inutile de déménager. Allez voir votre propriétaire et demandez-lui d'augmenter son loyer. »
  Pierre Doris

- « Le travail est l'opium du peuple… Je ne veux pas mourir drogué ! »
  Boris Vian

- « S'habiller est un mode de vie »
  Yves Saint Laurent

Also available as Kolibri Languages PRACTICAL GUIDES TO LIFESTYLE, MANNERS AND LANGUAGE

EATING AND SHOPPING IN FRANCE
Pam Bourgeois

In EATING AND SHOPPING IN FRANCE, you will discover everything you need to know to enable you to eat well and do your shopping in France. Cultural tips, historical anecdotes, useful words and expressions, amusing idioms, quizzes and key information will help you understand the French way of life.

- Discover the polite way to cut French cheeses.
- Learn why Marseille is associated with soap.
- Discover the differences between a Parisian brasserie and a 'bouchon' in Lyon.
- Learn key vocabulary for talking about wine.
- Prepare yourself for shopping in French markets with key information.
- Know what to expect when you go into traditional French food shops.

EATING AND SHOPPING IN FRANCE will help you prepare your trip and will be a unique souvenir when you return home.

ISBN : 979-10-91624-00-8

www.kolibrilanguages.com

MEETING THE FRENCH
Pam Bourgeois

In MEETING THE FRENCH, you will find everything you need to know when meeting French people, whether formally or informally. Cultural tips, historical anecdotes, useful words and expressions, amusing idioms, quizzes and key information will help you understand the French way of life.

- Find out what to expect if you are invited for an *apéritif* or a meal.
- Discover French wedding traditions.
- Know when to use *tu* or *vous*.
- Understand regional differences.
- Learn how to talk about the weather, everyday life and even politics.
- Gain valuable insights into the French sense of humour.

MEETING THE FRENCH will help you prepare your trip and will be a unique souvenir when you return home.

ISBN : 979-10-91624-04-6

www.kolibrilanguages.com

Photo credits

p5 top: Patrick Wang / Shutterstock.com
p7 bottom left: Kari Masson
p9 centre: Kari Masson
p10 bottom: Penelope Jordan
p11 top left: Nicole Fash
p13 top left: Kari Masson
p14: Nicole Fash
p16 top: Tupungato / Shutterstock.com
p18 top: Tupungato / Shutterstock.com
p20 bottom left: Eric Fahrner / Shutterstock.com
p22 left: Kari Masson
p24 top: Nola Rin / Shutterstock.com
p24 bottom: Kari Masson
p29 right: Christian Wilkinson / Shutterstock.com
p32 top: Spirit of America / Shutterstock.com
p32 centre: Unclesam / Fotolia.com
p32 bottom: Naty Strawberry / Fotolia.com
p33 top: aragami12345s / Shutterstock.com
p35 bottom: CJC / Fotolia.com
p37 top right: nui7711 / Shutterstock.com
p37 bottom left: Ken Ziegler
p44 bottom left: Olga Besnard / Shutterstock.com
p46 top: Radu Razvan / Shutterstock.com
p46 bottom: Rostislav Glinsky / Shutterstock.com
p49 top: elen_studio / Shutterstock.com
p51 top: Elena Elisseeva / Shutterstock.com

p51 bottom left: Kesu / Shutterstock.com
p56 top left: Alain Lauga / Shutterstock.com
p56 right: Ken Ziegler
p57 top: fstockfoto / Shutterstock.com
p57 centre: Solovyova Lyudmyla / Shutterstock.com
p57 bottom: Chantal de Bruijne / Shutterstock.com
p58 bottom left: Ferenc Szelepcsenyi / Shutterstock.com
p58 bottom left: Frédéric Prochasson / Fotolia.com
p62 left: Prometheus72 / Shutterstock.com
p64 top: Ignatius Wooster / Fotolia
p64 bottom left: Picture Catcher / Fotolia
p76 bottom right: Nadejda Ivanova / Shutterstock.com
p80 top: Djama / Fotolia.com
p84 right: Jean-Marie Bel / LinguaProduction sarl
p86 bottom: Gubin Yury / Shutterstock.com
p89 right: Anton Oparin / Shutterstock.com
p90 right: Anton Oparin / Shutterstock.com
p91 right: Anton Oparin / Shutterstock.com
p92 top: PCruciatti / Shutterstock.com
p92-93: Tupungato / Shutterstock.com
p93 centre: Charlie Edward / Shutterstock.com
p94 right: Anton Oparin / Shutterstock.com
p95 right: Anton Oparin / Shutterstock.com

Front cover, top: Mihai-Bogdan Lazar / Shutterstock.com
Front cover, bottom right: Kari Masson

© Pam Bourgeois, 2013
publié par Kolibri Languages (département de LinguaProduction sarl)
Les Meules, 69640 Cogny - France

Tous droits de reproduction, de traduction et d'adaptation réservés pour tous pays.

Toute reproduction ou représentation intégrale ou partielle, par quelque procédé que ce soit, sans l'autorisation de l'auteur ou de ses ayants droit, du texte contenu dans le présent ouvrage et qui est la propriété de l'auteur est strictement interdite.
LIFE IN FRANCE
ISBN : 979-10-91624-08-4

Dépôt légal : avril 2013
Imprimé en France (Printed in France) avril 2013
par Chevillon Imprimeur, 26 boulevard Kennedy, 89100 Sens

Life in France